Get the most from this book

Everyone has to decide his or her own revision strategy, but it is essential to review your work, learn it and test your understanding. These Revision Notes will help you to do that in a planned way, topic by topic. Use this book as the cornerstone of your revision and don't hesitate to write in it – personalise your notes and check your progress by ticking off each section as you revise.

Tick to track your progress

Use the revision planner on page 4 to plan your revision, topic by topic. Tick each box when you have:
- revised and understood a topic
- tested yourself
- practised the exam questions and checked your answers.

You can also keep track of your revision by ticking off each topic heading in the book. You may find it helpful to add your own notes as you work through each topic.

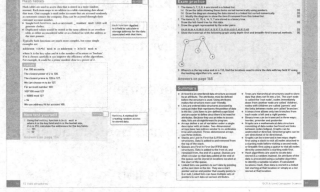

Features to help you succeed

Exam tips

Expert tips are given throughout the book to help you polish your exam technique in order to maximise your chances in the exam.

Now test yourself

These short, knowledge-based questions provide the first step in testing your learning. Answers are at the back of the book.

Definitions and key words

Clear, concise definitions of essential key terms are provided where they first appear.

Key words from the specification are highlighted in purple throughout the book.

Revision activities

These activities will help you to understand each topic in an interactive way.

Exam practice

Practice exam questions are provided for each topic. Use them to consolidate your revision and practise your exam skills. Answers are at the back of the book.

Summaries

The summaries provide a quick-check bullet list for each topic.

A Level only

This marker means the content is only needed for the full A level exam.

My revision planner

1 Computational thinking

   7 Computational thinking

  11 Elements of computational thinking

2 Problem solving

  16 Problem solving

  18 Programming techniques

  26 Algorithms

3 Computer systems

  37 Types of programming language

  46 Software

  52 Applications generation

  55 Software development

  60 Computer systems

  66 Data types

  74 Computer arithmetic

  82 Data structures

  98 Logic gates and Boolean algebra

 105 Databases

 119 Data transmission

 131 The internet

4 Legal, ethical, moral and social issues

 138 Computer law and ethical, moral and social issues

 149 **Now test yourself answers**

 157 **Exam practice answers**

REVISED   TESTED   EXAM READY

Countdown to my exams

6–8 weeks to go

- Start by looking at the specification – make sure you know exactly what material you need to revise and the style of the examination. Use the revision planner on page 4 to familiarise yourself with the topics.
- Organise your notes, making sure you have covered everything on the specification. The revision planner will help you to group your notes into topics.
- Work out a realistic revision plan that will allow you time for relaxation. Set aside days and times for all the subjects that you need to study, and stick to your timetable.
- Set yourself sensible targets. Break your revision down into focused sessions of around 40 minutes, divided by breaks. These Revision Notes organise the basic facts into short, memorable sections to make revising easier.

REVISED ☐

2–6 weeks to go

- Read through the relevant sections of this book and refer to the exam tips, exam summaries and key words. Tick off the topics as you feel confident about them. Highlight those topics you find difficult and look at them again in detail.
- Test your understanding of each topic by working through the 'Now test yourself' questions in the book. Look up the answers at the back of the book.
- Make a note of any problem areas as you revise, and ask your teacher to go over these in class.
- Look at past papers. They are one of the best ways to revise and practise your exam skills. Write or prepare planned answers to the exam practice questions provided in this book. Check your answers at the back of the book.
- Use the revision activities to try out different revision methods. For example, you can make notes using mind maps, spider diagrams or flash cards.
- Track your progress using the revision planner and give yourself a reward when you have achieved your target.

REVISED ☐

1 week to go

- Try to fit in at least one more timed practice of an entire past paper and seek feedback from your teacher, comparing your work closely with the mark scheme.
- Check the revision planner to make sure you haven't missed out any topics. Brush up on any areas of difficulty by talking them over with a friend or getting help from your teacher.
- Attend any revision classes put on by your teacher. Remember, he or she is an expert at preparing people for examinations.

REVISED ☐

The day before the examination

- Flick through these Revision Notes for useful reminders, for example the exam tips, exam summaries and key terms.
- Check the time and place of your examination.
- Make sure you have everything you need – extra pens and pencils, tissues, a watch, bottled water, sweets.
- Allow some time to relax and have an early night to ensure you are fresh and alert for the examinations.

REVISED ☐

My exams

AS level Computer Science paper

Date:..

Time:..

Location:..

A level Computer Science paper

Date:..

Time:..

Location:..

Topic 1 Computational thinking

1 Computational thinking

Computer professionals have developed techniques to solve real-world problems and turn them into computer solutions. Computational thinking is making use of these techniques to solve problems with or without using a computer.

At its heart, computational thinking is changing a messy problem into something that can be:
- understood
- formally represented and solved.

Computational thinking is important because some of the biggest problems that people face are difficult to understand. Writing software is also difficult. The hope is that lessons learned from producing software can be applied more widely to provide solutions.

Mathematical approaches

REVISED

Traditionally, many problems have been solved successfully by applying mathematics, often in conjunction with known physical laws.

> **Examples**
>
> Here are some examples of problems that are solvable by mathematical and physical approaches:
> - plotting a course to the moon
> - predicting eclipses
> - estimating the amount of steel necessary to build a new model of car to a given specification.

In all the cases in these examples, it is feasible to acquire enough data to apply calculations and expect a reasonably accurate solution.

Difficulties arise if the:
- quality of the data is substandard
- maths applied does not represent reality.

However, we would normally expect a new plane to fly, even if there are teething problems; the physics is known and the maths has been applied before.

Messy problems

REVISED

Many problems that need to be solved are much less likely to be amenable to a reliable solution. Not all problems can be neatly described. This is because the:
- underlying issues are not understood
- data is not sufficient
- data is erroneous
- underlying issues are excessively complex.

Often, messy problems cause trouble because people think that they understand them. False confidence has often led to bad solutions that do not solve a problem or in fact make things worse. There are academic specialities that are founded on non-scientific grounds.

Example

The stock market might fall spectacularly one day. It might bounce back the next. 'Experts' will happily explain why this happened. Perhaps a company Chief Executive made an announcement on profits or interest rates changed.

What no one can ever do is say what the market will do tomorrow.

Example

Other messy problem domains include:
- biological systems
- ecological systems
- climate
- societies.

In all the cases above, the complexity defeats normal scientific and mathematical solution. Climatologists make claims about future climate change but cannot predict next Friday's weather. In each of these cases, models of the atmosphere are used and the reliability of the models may not always be as good as hoped for because the reality of the atmosphere is extremely complex. The outcomes will depend on the quantity and quality of the data available.

Help in solving messy problems will probably come from computational thinking. It already has in many cases. One classic example is the use of shotgun sequencing algorithms to piece together the structure of the human genome by repeatedly matching the overlapping segments of genes that have been broken into fragments.

> **Revision activity**
>
> List a few messy problems that it might be possible to solve if you had enough data. Include personal as well as large-scale issues.

Breaking down problems

REVISED

Increasingly, difficult problems are being solved by applying **algorithms**. Algorithms can be helpful because:
- teaching a problem-solving approach to a computer helps in understanding the problem
- algorithmic solutions can be executed quickly by modern computer systems
- it is possible to resort to trial and error.

> **Algorithm** A set of instructions to achieve a given task.

Computational thinking is algorithmic thinking. It requires the following stages:

1 **Understand the problem:** This can be a serious stumbling block. How do we know that we understand a problem sufficiently?
2 **Formulate the problem:** Produce a concise representation of the problem. This will normally involve abstraction and some form of mathematical notation.
3 **Design an algorithm:** Once a clear representation of the problem is obtained, set about designing algorithms to apply to the representation.
4 **Implement the algorithm:** Write a program that implements the algorithm.
5 **Run the code and solve the original problem:** Actually try it out. After this, it is necessary to evaluate the results to see if they have solved the problem.

(a) **Abstraction:** Central to this process is the idea of abstraction. This means turning reality into a model that can be processed. With big problems, this requires another fundamental approach: decomposition.

(b) **Decomposition:** Decomposition has long been part of the computer scientist's toolbox. The top–down approach is a popular and successful way to produce complex computer systems. It has the advantage that big problems become many small problems that are easier to formulate into solutions.

Hierarchies are often produced to help generate a solution.

Top-down problem solving

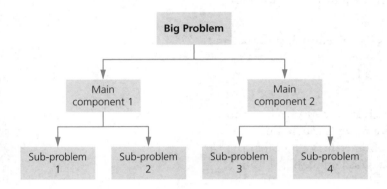

Figure 1.1 A tree hierarchical structure

> **Top-down problem solving**
> An approach to problem solving that involves starting with the 'big picture'. This is then broken down (decomposed) into sub-problems that may be represented as 'black boxes', where the detail is left until later.

> **Example**
>
> The internet is an example of a spectacularly successful computer implementation. One reason for its success is that its parts have been decomposed to sub-problems such as:
> - protocols
> - packet-switching techniques
> - common standards
> - layering.

> **Example**
>
> Developers of database systems make use of decomposition at various stages of the process, using:
> - data-flow diagrams to model the components of the system
> - Jackson diagrams to model the processes needed
> - entity-relationship diagrams to determine the links between data entities.

Structured programming

Successful programs follow certain patterns and processes that have become part of computational thinking. Structured programming is a way of dividing a large program into modules. Each module typically solves one problem and the modules are then put together.

This approach has been aided by the realisation that all programs tend to consist of just three constructs:

1 sequence

2 selection

3 iteration.

(See pages 18–19.)

Object-oriented programming

Object-oriented programming is another way in which decomposition is routinely used to solve programming problems. Objects (see page 42) consist of isolated program units containing code and data. These are built together to form a complete solution. The objects are another example of abstraction and can be reused with or without modification (see 'inheritance' on page 43).

Algorithms

REVISED

The aim of writing algorithms is to produce a process that will work on a generalised representation of a problem; that is, it can be reused for similar problems.

It is not straightforward to produce algorithms. We need to ensure that an algorithm is:

● correct
● efficient.

Proving that an algorithm is incorrect can be trivial; we just need to show that, in just one case, it fails. Proving that it is correct is much more difficult and requires mathematical induction. Sometimes a problem is 'too hard'. We then need to decide if there is a 'good enough' solution that is acceptable.

Exam practice

1 Describe three human problem-solving activities that can be solved reasonably accurately with mathematical techniques. [6]
2 Describe three messy human problems or dilemmas that might be solved at least in part using computational techniques. [6]
3 Explain the top-down approach to problem solving. [2]
4 (a) Explain the term 'abstraction'. [3]
  (b) State two examples of how decomposition can assist a systems developer. [2]

Answers on page 157

Summary

● Computational thinking is using the techniques of computer scientists to tackle problems.
● The techniques have developed from the advances of computer science but are applicable to many other problem domains as well.
● Also, computational methodology has been extended to provide solutions to many new problems, using computation by machine as well as incorporating human creativity.
● Some problems are amenable to completely computed solutions. Others are better solved by a partnership of human and machine.
● Problems can only be solved if the nature of the problem is properly understood and there is enough data to work with.
● Decomposition and abstraction are key elements of successful problem solving

using computational methods. In particular, abstraction allows solutions to be tried out virtually before money and effort is committed to a real-life solution.
● Ultimately, algorithms are used to solve problems. Understanding how to formulate and improve these is central to computational thinking.
● Much of the progress made in computing solutions in recent years has been more to do with producing better algorithms than better hardware.
● Computational thinking should be applied to your coursework as well as to many of the problems that you will encounter while studying computer science and in the written exam papers.

2 Elements of computational thinking

Computability is something that is not affected by the speed and power of a machine. It can be demonstrated that there is no computable solution to some problems.

However, algorithms are often applied to new and unexpected situations.

Some useful solutions or estimates can sometimes be made that are 'good enough'. A useful solution to a messy problem may sometimes be achieved by combining computed 'solutions' with human insight.

There are certain well-defined thinking approaches that can be deployed in solving problems in a helpful way. (Chapter 3 looks at the typical stages of problem solving.)

Some well-known computational techniques can be carried straight across to real-world problem solving.

Backtracking

Some problems are best solved by trying out a sequence of actions and determining how far they succeed until it becomes apparent that it can go no further. Backtracking is essentially trial and error. It is used extensively in some program approaches.

> **Revision activity**
>
> Get hold of a Prolog compiler and try a few simple programs that make use of backtracking.

Example

Debugging a program

Iterative program testing is a common way to proceed when developing a program. It is useful to save each version of a program then, if an error is introduced, it is possible to go back to the last saved working version and start again from there.

If a program statement produces an error, it can be useful to go backwards through the code, checking each statement that has an effect on the outcome of the failed line. This can reduce the number of statements that need to be re-examined compared with starting from the beginning. Debugging software often provides facilities to do this.

Example

Backtracking is carried out mentally when planning a chess move. A possible move is considered and then the consequences of that move. If the consequence is bad, then you go back and re-examine possible moves until an alternative with a desirable outcome is found.

Applying backtracking can be complex. In computational terms, recursion can be used to try out alternative paths.

Data mining

REVISED

Some applications of computing lead to new insights. Data mining examines large data sets looking for patterns and relationships. Databases are designed to store and process data in predefined ways. When they get large enough, unexpected relationships may be uncovered, especially if other databases are examined as part of the same process.

Data mining incorporates:
- cluster analysis
- pattern matching
- anomaly detection
- regression analysis.

Revision activity

Research online some examples of data mining. In particular, look for cases where unexpected results have surfaced from the analysis of big data stores.

One particularly interesting and unexpected case is to be found in the analysis of baseball statistics: www.slideshare.net/ salfordsystems/data-mining-for-baseball-new-ppt-11489806.

Performance modelling

REVISED

Performance modelling is another use of models in computational thinking.

Real-life objects and systems, as well as computer software, can be modelled in order to predict how they will behave when in use.

Performance can depend on complexity. This can be assessed by analysing program functions and using the Big-O notation to show how algorithms behave with increasing size of input.

Simulations can be used to predict performance before real systems are constructed.

Pipelining

REVISED

Pipelining is a common computing technique where the output of one process can be fed into another.

Complex jobs can be divided up into separate pipelines so that parallel processing can occur.

This technique parallels real-life situations such as assembly-line processing.

Visualisation

REVISED

Problems and data can often be better understood when translated into a visual model. An old example is any type of graph, which often conveys trends better than the raw data used to draw it.

Computers have facilitated many new and inventive ways to visualise situations. Often, these show unexpected and interesting trends that could not be produced by traditional manual methods.

Example

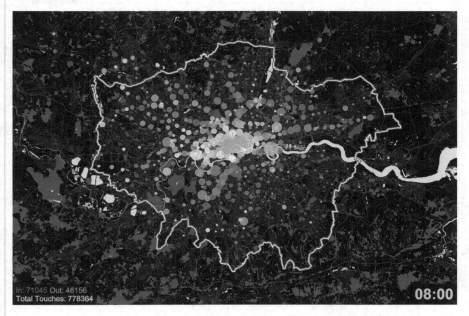

In: 71045 Out: 46156
Total Touches: 778364

08:00

Figure 2.1 **Visualisation of Oyster card use on the London Underground**

Thinking abstractly

REVISED

Computational thinking requires abstraction.

Abstraction is a representation of reality. It requires recognising what is important in a problem, then devising a means effectively to code it – to write it down and formulate it in a way that can be passed to an algorithm.

In computing, we use abstractions extensively. We can also use them to help solve problems without using computers.

Examples

Examples of abstractions:
- variables
- objects
- layers
- data models
- data structures
- entity-relation diagrams.

Thinking ahead

REVISED

In computing, thinking ahead involves planning inputs and outputs. It is useful to apply this approach to other problems; for example, by asking:
- What answers do we need?
- What do we need to know or have before we can get what we need?

Caching

This is an illustration of 'thinking ahead'. A cache is a temporary store where instructions or data that are likely to be needed are anticipated and are stored, ready for fast access. Cached data can replace the need for recalculation or slow access of data stored online or on disk.

Revision activity

Imagine you have a presentation to do for an interview. What inputs do you need? What should you put into the presentation? How do you know?

Thinking procedurally

REVISED

Computer programs are designed and written in modules.

When writing programs, we generally think of algorithms expressed as sequences of instructions. These are often packaged up into modules for ease of writing.

1 Divide up a problem into sub-problems.
2 Do solutions already exist for any of the sub-problems?
3 How do the sub-problems interact with each other?

Thinking logically

REVISED

Thinking logically requires you to infer things from what you know. In programming, it requires understanding where decisions need to be made and their consequences.

To think logically when solving a problem, it is necessary to:
● identify when decision making is required
● identify what decisions need to be made
● identify the test conditions to enable a decision to be made
● understand the interactions between decisions
● apply decision making to the real-world problem.

A Level only

Thinking concurrently

REVISED

Sometimes it can be more efficient to step outside and think of how a job might be done better if some parts were performed at the same time as others; that is, concurrently. This can affect the algorithms we make.

If we have more resources, such as parallel processors, we can divide up jobs to be performed at the same time.

Exam practice

1 Describe how visualisation could be used to demonstrate the preferred routes of drivers commuting from the suburbs into a city. [2]
2 Describe how backtracking could be used to locate lost keys. [2]
3 (a) To what extent is choosing a career computable? [2]
   (b) What data would be helpful to the process? [2]
4 A young man is given £50 000 in shares in a company. He could cash them now and pay his university fees or he could leave them and possibly gain £1 000 000 in ten years' time. What questions should he ask so that he can make a sensible decision? [3]
5 Give examples of how thinking concurrently could be useful in planning the design of a restaurant. [3]
6 Describe how caching can be used to make a computer program more efficient. [3]
7 A shuffled pack of playing cards is to be sorted into four suits.
   (a) Draw a flowchart to plan how this could be done. [4]
   (b) Imagine you have someone to help you. How might you use this extra help to speed up the process? [2]
   (c) How would you determine whether the extra help saved time? [2]

Answers on pages 157–58

Summary

- Computational thinking has been extensively analysed in recent years. Some general principles have emerged that make the problem-solving process easier to understand and provide useful pointers as to how best to proceed when tackling a problem or project.
- Backtracking has long been understood and used in declarative programming languages such as Prolog. The approach has a useful wider application.
- New approaches have developed that lead to new discoveries. Data mining was an unconventional approach to database analysis when it first appeared, but it is now realised that large and unpredictable data stores can be processed to reveal unexpected insights.
- The most often quoted constituents of computational thinking are summarised as:
  - thinking abstractly
  - thinking ahead
  - thinking logically
  - thinking concurrently
  - thinking procedurally
  - thinking recursively.
- All these ideas spring from computer science in practice and they can usefully be referred to as helpful approaches when looking at new problems.

Topic 2 Problem solving

3 Problem solving

Problems come in various guises but there are two main divisions:
- **well-defined problems**
- **ill-defined problems**.

> **Well-defined problems** Problems that are clear to understand. Their solutions have defined expectations. It is possible to follow clear pathways to plan the solutions.
>
> **Ill-defined problems** Messy problems. It is not always clear what is required to solve them or even what the goals of solving them are. They cannot be solved by following a clearly defined recipe. They require human creativity.

Some problems consist of a mix of these two main types. Often it is possible to divide them into parts, some of which can be solved in a generic way and others that require insight.

Problem solving is not always an end in itself. It can be part of a wider quest to improve all sorts of situations such as building a better car or making better weather forecasts.

> **Revision activity**
>
> Very quickly, think of one example each of a well-defined problem and an ill-defined one.

Stages of problem solving

REVISED

When solving a problem, there are stages that are helpful to go through.

1 Understand the problem

You cannot begin to solve a problem unless you know what you are trying to solve.
- Do you have all the data you need to understand it? If not, can you get the information you need?
- Is the problem possibly unsolvable?
- Could you solve just some of the problem and still be better off?
- Is it possible to divide the problem into sub–problems?

2 Devise a plan

Make a list of things to do.
- Are there patterns that could allow generic or repeated use of solutions?
- Can maths help?
- Look at similar problems and their solutions. Has this problem been solved before? Can I learn from what has previously been solved?

3 Carry out the plan

- Check that what you are doing is in fact correct.
- Ask the questions 'Am I doing the right thing?' and 'Am I doing it right?'

4 Review your work

Look back over what you have done.

- Can your solution be improved? For example, are the algorithms the most efficient that you could use?
- Is any of the solution reusable in the future?
- Is the problem effectively solved?

Heuristics

Don't forget that some problems need very precise and reliable solutions. Others can make do with 'good enough' solutions. It is not always worth the effort to make a perfect solution.

Exam practice

1 Classify the following problems according to whether they are solvable by (A) generic methods, (B) creative insight or (C) a mixture of both.
  (a) How much paint do I need to decorate my lounge? [1]
  (b) What is the cheapest way to fly to New York? [1]
  (c) Which holiday is likely to be enjoyed by all the family? [1]
  (d) Which course should I take at university? [1]
  (e) Should I even go to university? [1]
2 A publisher wants to produce a revision guide like this one. It costs more to produce more pages.
  It is important to get it to the market on time. It must make a profit or at least lead to increased sales of another product.
  (a) List the sub-problems that might be addressed in solving this problem. [4]
  (b) For each sub-problem, discuss the role of defined or heuristic approaches. [8]

Answers on page 159

> **Revision activity**
>
> We are often told that prejudice is a bad thing, or we are scolded for being 'judgemental'.
>
> To what extent is this a sensible criticism of heuristics? Should we be prejudiced against prejudice?

Summary

- It is necessary to understand a problem before it is possible to solve it.
- Some problems are clear cut.
- Others are messy – normally ones where human activity or a complex system is involved.
- There are well-documented, tried and tested stages for solving problems that are best followed when faced with a new situation.
- These incorporate understanding what you need to do and what you need to have available before a solution is possible.
- Consideration is needed of whether a problem is in fact solvable at all or whether it may be partially solvable. Some problems will never be solved. Some solutions bring enough benefit for them to be 'good enough' and still worth pursuing.
- Heuristics are not to be neglected. A 'rule of thumb' is often a good way to approach a problem in order to find a likely way forward without spending too much initial effort on analysis that may take you in the wrong direction.

4 Programming techniques

Programming constructs

REVISED

Programs are built from standard components, many of which have not changed in principle for many years. There are three fundamental constructs: sequence, selection and iteration.

1 Sequence

A sequence is a series of statements that are executed one after another. Most code for most computers is like this.

2 Selection

Selection is where a decision is made based on the state of a Boolean expression. Program control is diverted to another part of the program according to whether the expression evaluates to 'true' or 'false'.

> **Example**
>
> ```
> if a>b then new_function()
> ```
>
> Selection is achieved with high-level statements such as:
>
> ```
> if..then
> switch..case
> ```

> **Example**
>
> ```
> if (condition)
> {
> call function;
> }
> ```

> **Example**
>
> ```
> if answer in("A", "a"):
>     write_file()
> elif answer in ("R", "r")
>     read_file()
> ```

Assembly language uses branch instructions such as BRA (branch always), or BRP (branch if the value in the accumulator is positive).

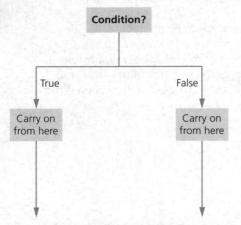

Figure 4.2 A decision with a Boolean expression

Figure 4.1 A sequence

3 Iteration

Iteration means repetition. It is used to make a section of code repeat itself. The repeated section is called a 'loop'.

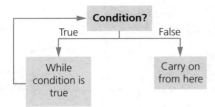

Figure 4.3 Using a Boolean expression to repeat code

Boolean expressions are again often used to determine whether to operate a repeat.

There are several standard ways to control iteration. The syntax varies according to programming language but the principles are the same in each case.

Condition tested at end of loop

Commonly this is implemented by a **repeat..until** structure. It means keep doing something until a condition is met. These loops are always executed at least once.

Condition tested at the start of a loop

This is usually written as **while..do** or **while..endwhile** or **while** followed by an indent. These loops may or may not be executed as if the condition fails, they will not even be entered.

Count controlled loops

This is written in a variety of ways such as

```
for i in range(0, 3):
   print (i)
```

or

```
For index As Integer = 1 To 5
   Debug.Write(index)
Next
```

'For' loops are used when it is known in advance how many iterations are required.

Recursion

REVISED

This is where a procedure or function calls itself. It is another way of producing iteration. Recursion will cause a stack overflow error if a terminating condition is not built in. The following python code is an example.

Example

```
def recurse(number):
   print(number)
   number+=1
   recurse(number)  ←——— function calls itself here
   return;

recurse(1)
```

Now test yourself

TESTED

1 What would happen if the example code on page 19 was executed?
2 How could you fix the problem?

Answers on page 149

Variables

REVISED

All non-trivial programs use variables.

Variables are named locations that store data in which the contents can be changed during program execution.

Variables are assigned a data type (see from page 66). How this happens depends on the programming language you are using. In some languages, the data type may be declared; that is, assigned by an explicit statement, for example:

```
int count;
char letter;
char name[30];
```

Other languages may assign a data type by its first use, for example, **number=1** sets number as an integer. In some languages, the data type may be changed dynamically during program execution.

Data type is important. It determines what you can do with a variable. For example, you can't sensibly add characters together.

> **Example**
>
> This Python code sets up the variables 'a' and 'b' as strings.
> ```
> a='20'
> b='30'
> c=a+b
> print(c)
> ```
> The output is 2030 which may not be as intended.

Functions usually expect certain data types. Give them the wrong type and unexpected results will occur.

Global and local variables

Global variables can be 'seen' throughout a program. They are declared or set outside any functions or subprograms.

Local variables are set or declared inside a function or other subprogram. They can only be accessed from within that subprogram.

Global variables can be dangerous. It is easy to overlook when they are changed.

Functions and procedures

Programs are written in separate subsections. This makes it easier to create and test them.

Subprograms are variously named but they are all self-contained units of code that perform some well-defined purpose.

Functions are subprograms that usually, but not always, return a value.

Procedures perform some operation but do not return a value.

As well as providing a means of writing functions, most programming languages are supplied with built-in functions. For example in Python 3.0 `print()` is a function where what is to be printed is supplied inside the brackets, such as `print('hello world')`.

Parameter passing

REVISED

Subprograms usually require data to be sent to them so that they can be reused. The supplied data is called a parameter. In the case of the recursive function:

```
def recurse(number):
   print(number)
   number+=1
   recurse(number)
   return;

recurse(1)
```

'number' is the parameter. The function requires a number to be supplied to it. In this example it is initially 1.

Parameters can be passed by **reference**. This means that the address of the variable is passed to the subprogram. In this case, if the variable is changed by the function, it stays changed.

Reference The data passed is the address of the variable.

Here are some examples written in VBA.

Example

Parameter passing by reference:

```
Sub Button1_Click()
Dim x As Integer
x = 10

MsgBox ref_ex(x)
MsgBox (x)
End Sub

Function ref_ex(ByRef x As Integer) As Integer
x = x * 4
ref_ex = x
End Function
```

This is the output from the function:

Followed by the output of the variable:

Microsoft Excel	X
40	
OK	

Microsoft Excel	X
40	
OK	

The original value of x has been changed from 10 to 40.

Parameters can be passed by **value**. This means that a copy of the variable is passed to the subprogram. In this case, the original variable is unchanged by the function.

Value The data passed is a copy of the variable.

Example

```
Sub Button1_Click()
Dim x As Integer
x = 10

MsgBox val_ex(x)
MsgBox (x)
End Sub
Function val_ex(ByVal x As Integer) As Integer
x = x * 4
val_ex = x
End Function
```

The function works on a copy.

This outputs this from the function:

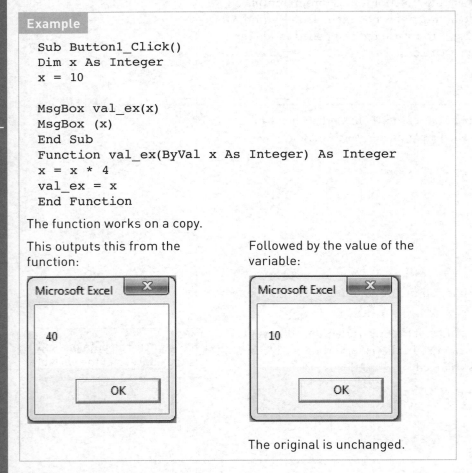

Microsoft Excel

40

OK

Followed by the value of the variable:

Microsoft Excel

10

OK

The original is unchanged.

Writing programs

Programmers write programs in a programming language. What they write is called source code. To write and save source code you need an editor.

```
File  Edit  Format  Run  Options  Windows  Help
def recurse(number):
    print(number)
    number+=1
    if number<20:
       recurse(number)
    return;

recurse(1)
```

Figure 4.4 **Program source code in an editor**

Source code will not run on the processor, it has to be translated.

Assembly language source code is translated by an assembler into an object-code file.

High-level languages are translated by either a compiler or an interpreter:
- a compiler that produces an object-code file

or
- an interpreter that runs each line of the program as it is translated.

4 Programming techniques

Translator	Result
Compiler	Produces an object-code file. This can be run directly from the operating system.
Interpreter	Does not produce an object-code file; it translates and executes the translated program line by line.
	The interpreter must be present every time the program is run.

Compiled object code is usually produced as a number of separate modules.
- The modules must be joined together to form the completed program.
- The completed program is an **executable** file.
- Software called a **linker** does the joining.

> **Executable** A program file that can be run directly from the operating system.
>
> **Linker** Software that joins a number of object code files and consolidates them into a single runnable program.

The IDE

REVISED

An IDE (Integrated Development Environment) contains all the tools needed to write, develop and debug a program. A typical IDE has the following tools:
- an editor, probably with formatting help facilities
- a build facility, to automate the whole process of constructing a program from its component parts
- a debugger.

Debugging usually allows the programmer to inspect variables, by stopping the program execution at some point.

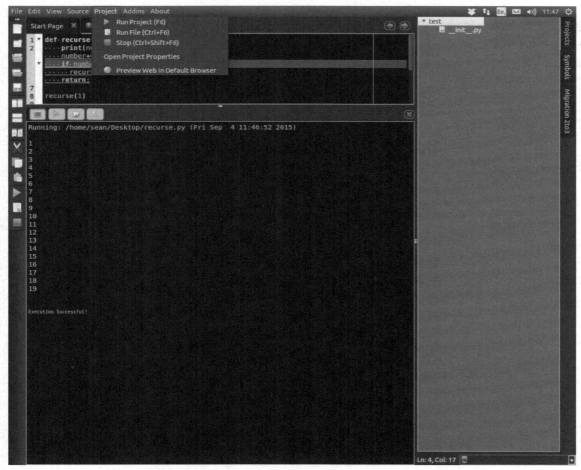

Figure 4.5 Source code being tested in an IDE.

Revision activity

Get hold of at least two IDEs, preferably that can be used with your usual programming language.

For each one, find out the facilities that it offers the programmer.

Try some of these out on a program that you have written.

Object-oriented techniques

REVISED

Objects are described in Chapter 6.

Many programs are written using objects.

Objects are self-contained units that include:
● methods (code)
● properties (data about the object).

Objects are derived from classes.
● Classes are a generalised plan for a group of objects.
● Classes allow inheritance.
● Inheritance refers to different objects having similar functionality, inherited from the class definition.

Objects allow encapsulation. This means isolating the object from others. The contents of an object are hidden from the outside which avoids unexpected interactions.

Exam practice

1 Describe how a Boolean expression can control the operation of a loop.   [4]
2 Describe the difference between a 'while loop' and a 'for loop'.   [2]
3 Explain the dangers of using global variables.   [2]
4 In terms of a function, explain what a parameter is.   [1]
5 Explain the differences between passing parameters by reference and by value.   [4]
6 Explain the difference between a class and an object.   [2]

Answers on page 159

Summary

- To a large extent, programming as a craft has not changed much for a long time.
- Many new techniques continually appear, but still programs are made up of components that use three basic constructs:
  - sequence
  - selection
  - iteration.
- Iteration (looping) itself is commonly implemented in four standard ways:
  - condition tested on entry to loop
  - condition tested at end of loop
  - count controlled loop
  - recursion.
- Programs all make use of variables. These are either locally or globally defined and used. There are issues concerned with the best way to use these.
- Programs should normally be modular. This is part of the lesson we learn from decomposition and thinking procedurally.
- Modularity is achieved by using procedures, functions and objects. These modules normally receive and give back data as parameters.
- Objects are built from classes, and like other modules help to produce reusable code.
- Parameters can be passed by value or by reference. It is important to realise what you are doing in order to get the results you expect.
- Writing programs in high-level languages or in assembly language usually requires software tools such as:
  - an editor
  - a translator (compiler, interpreter or assembler)
  - a linker.
- These and other tools are usually provided packaged together in an IDE (Integrated Development Environment).
- The other tools include facilities to debug and package the program.

5 Algorithms

This chapter covers a number of searching, sorting and route finding algorithms.

Search algorithms

Linear search

Linear search involves methodically searching one location after another until the searched-for value is found. The linear search algorithm starts at the beginning of a list and checks each item in turn until the desired item is found.

> **Example**
>
> If we are looking for E, the algorithm checks location 0 (D), location 1 (F), location 2 (C), location 3 (A) and then finds E at location 4.
>
> | D | F | C | A | E | B | H | G |
> |---|---|---|---|---|---|---|---|

It can be expressed in pseudocode as follows:

```
pointer=0
WHILE pointer<LengthOfList AND list[pointer]!=searchedFor
   Add one to pointer
ENDWHILE
IF pointer>=LengthOfList THEN
   PRINT("Item is not in the list")
ELSE
   PRINT("Item is at location "+pointer)
ENDIF
```

Binary search

Binary search works by dividing the list in two each time until the item being searched for is found. For binary search to work, the list has to be in order.

```
LowerBound=0
UpperBound=LengthOfList-1
Found=False
WHILE Found==False AND LowerBound!=UpperBound
   MidPoint=ROUND((LowerBound+UpperBound)/2)
   IF List[MidPoint]==searchedFor THEN
      Found=True
   ELSEIF List[MidPoint]<searchedFor THEN
      LowerBound=MidPoint+1
   ELSE
      UpperBound=MidPoint-1
   ENDIF
ENDWHILE
IF List[MidPoint]==searchedFor THEN
   PRINT("Item found at "+MidPoint)
ELSE
   PRINT("Item not in list")
ENDIF
```

Example

A	B	C	D	E	F	G	H	I	J	K	L	M	N	O
0	1	2	3	4	5	6	7	8	9	10	11	12	13	14

LB   MP   UB

- If we are searching for D in the list above, we start with the lower bound being the first location (0) and the upper bound being the last location (14). We find the midpoint by adding the locations together and dividing by 2. (0+14)/2 = 7.
- The midpoint value at 7 is H which is higher than D. This means the highest possible location it could be is 6 so we make the UB 6. (If the value had been lower than the one we are looking for then we could have deduced the lowest possible location is 8 and would have made this the LB.)
- The process is repeated until the MP is the value being sought.
- If the LB and UB become the same location and that location does not contain the item we are looking for, the item is not in the list.

Now test yourself

TESTED ☐

1 State the precondition needed for binary search.
2 Give the maximum number of locations that need to be checked for a:
   (a) linear search of 1000 items.
   (b) binary search of 1000 items.

Answers on page 149

Sorting algorithms

REVISED ☐

Four sorting algorithms are covered here: bubble sort, insertion sort, merge sort and quicksort.

Bubble sort

Bubble sort works as follows:

Create a Boolean variable called swapMade and set it to true.

```
Set swapMade to true
WHILE swapMade is true
  Set swapMade to false.
  Start at position 0.
  FOR position=0 TO listlength−2 i.e. the last but one position
    Compare the item at the position you are at
    with the one ahead of it.
    IF they are out of order THEN
      Swap items and set swapMade to true.
    END IF
  NEXT position
END WHILE
```

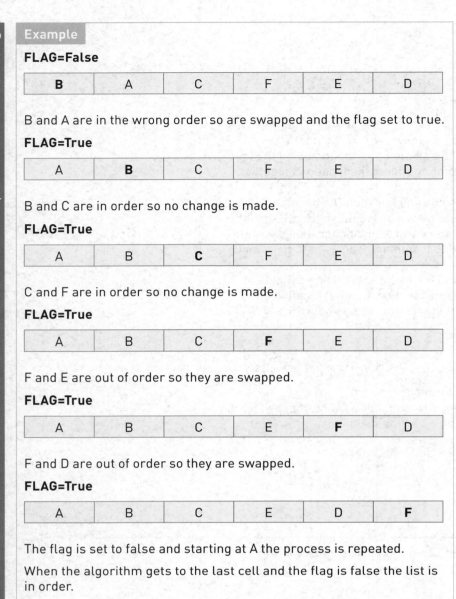

Example

FLAG=False

B	A	C	F	E	D

B and A are in the wrong order so are swapped and the flag set to true.

FLAG=True

A	B	C	F	E	D

B and C are in order so no change is made.

FLAG=True

A	B	C	F	E	D

C and F are in order so no change is made.

FLAG=True

A	B	C	F	E	D

F and E are out of order so they are swapped.

FLAG=True

A	B	C	E	F	D

F and D are out of order so they are swapped.

FLAG=True

A	B	C	E	D	F

The flag is set to false and starting at A the process is repeated.

When the algorithm gets to the last cell and the flag is false the list is in order.

Insertion sort

Insertion sort works by dividing a list into two parts: sorted and unsorted. Elements are inserted one by one into their correct position in the sorted section.

```
Make the first item the sorted list, the
remaining items are the unsorted list.
WHILE there are items in the unsorted list
    Take the first item of the unsorted list.
    WHILE there is an item to the left of it which
    is bigger than itself
        Swap with that item.
    END WHILE
    The sorted list is now one item bigger.
END WHILE
```

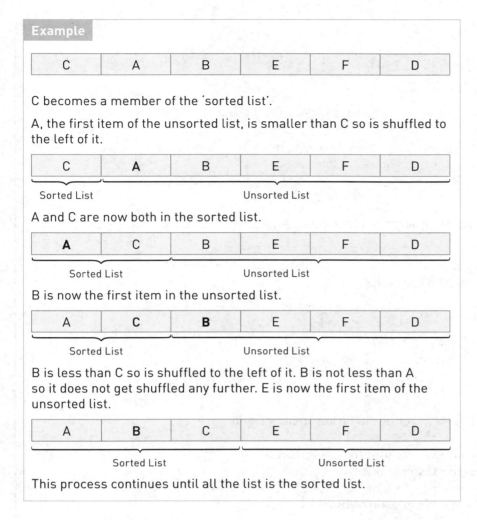

Example

| C | A | B | E | F | D |

C becomes a member of the 'sorted list'.

A, the first item of the unsorted list, is smaller than C so is shuffled to the left of it.

| C | A | B | E | F | D |

Sorted List | Unsorted List

A and C are now both in the sorted list.

| **A** | C | B | E | F | D |

Sorted List | Unsorted List

B is now the first item in the unsorted list.

| A | C | **B** | E | F | D |

Sorted List | Unsorted List

B is less than C so is shuffled to the left of it. B is not less than A so it does not get shuffled any further. E is now the first item of the unsorted list.

| A | **B** | C | E | F | D |

Sorted List | Unsorted List

This process continues until all the list is the sorted list.

Merge sort

A Level only

Merge sort splits a list of size *n* into *n* lists of size *1*. Each of these lists is merged with another. Each of the newly merged lists is merged with another. This is repeated until there is only one, sorted list. The key to this algorithm is the way the lists are merged. The following merging algorithm is used:

```
IF the first item in list1<the first item in list2
THEN
    Remove the first item from list1 and add it to
    newlist.
ELSE
    Remove the first item from list2 and add it to
    newlist.
ENDIF
ENDWHILE
IF list1 is empty THEN
    Add the remainder of list2 to newlist.
ELSE
    Add the remainder of list1 to newlist.
ENDIF
```

Example

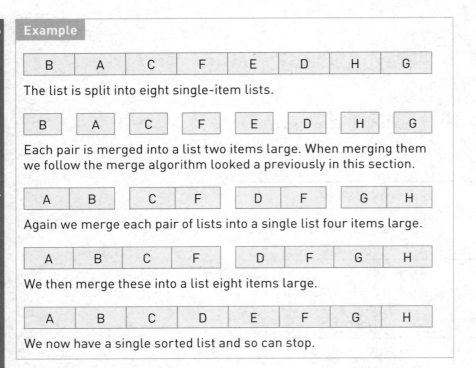

The list is split into eight single-item lists.

Each pair is merged into a list two items large. When merging them we follow the merge algorithm looked a previously in this section.

Again we merge each pair of lists into a single list four items large.

We then merge these into a list eight items large.

We now have a single sorted list and so can stop.

Quicksort

Quicksort works as follows:

1 Pick an item in the list and call it the pivot (it can be any item; we will always pick the first).
2 Split the remainder of the list into two sub-lists: those less than or equal to the pivot and those greater than the pivot.
3 Recursively apply step 2 until all sub-lists are pivots.
4 The pivots can now be combined to form a sorted list.

Example

Let's work through an example:

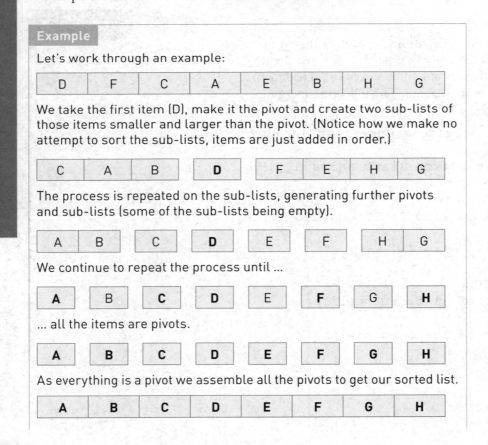

We take the first item (D), make it the pivot and create two sub-lists of those items smaller and larger than the pivot. (Notice how we make no attempt to sort the sub-lists, items are just added in order.)

The process is repeated on the sub-lists, generating further pivots and sub-lists (some of the sub-lists being empty).

We continue to repeat the process until …

… all the items are pivots.

As everything is a pivot we assemble all the pivots to get our sorted list.

This algorithm can be coded recursively. For large data sets this can require significant amounts of memory. To circumvent this there is an 'in-place' version:

```
Place leftPointer at first item in the list and
rightPointer at the last item in the list.
WHILE leftPointer!=rightPointer
   WHILE list[leftPointer] < list[rightPointer] AND
   leftPointer!=rightPointer
      Add one to leftPointer
   END WHILE
   Swap list[leftPointer] with list[rightPointer]
   WHILE list[leftPointer] < list[rightPointer] AND
   leftPointer!=rightPointer
      Subtract one from rightPointer
   END WHILE
   Swap list[leftPointer] with list[rightPointer]
END WHILE
```

Now the item pointed to by the left and right pointers is in order. We now apply the algorithm to the sub-lists either side of this item and continue this process until the whole list is sorted.

Now test yourself

TESTED

3 Describe how bubble sort works.
4 In quick sort, a pivot is picked. Explain what this pivot is used for.

Answers on page 149

Complexity

REVISED

We can compare algorithms in terms of their complexity. Complexity doesn't show us how fast an algorithm performs but rather how well it scales when given larger data sets to act upon.

We can use Big-O notation to denote an algorithm's worst case complexity. If we know the expression for the number of steps an algorithm takes to execute, we can get the Big-O expression by:
● removing all terms except the one with the largest exponent
● removing any constant factors.

Example

An algorithm takes $3n^2+4n-4$ steps.

Remove all terms except the one with the highest exponent:

$3n^2$

Remove any constant factors:

n^2

This gives a complexity of $O(n^2)$.

There are different classes of complexity:

Constant	O(1)
Logarithmic	O(log n)
Linear	O(n)
Polynomial	$O(n^k)$ Where k is a constant $> = 0$
Exponential	$O(k^n)$ Where k is constant > 1

Slowest growing

↓

Fastest growing

Shortest-path algorithms

REVISED

You need to know two shortest-path algorithms: Dijkstra's algorithm and A* search.

Dijkstra's algorithm

Dijkstra's algorithm finds the shortest path between two points and the algorithm goes as follows:

```
Mark the start node as a distance of 0 from
itself and all other nodes as an infinite
distance from the start node.
WHILE the destination node is unvisited
   Go to the closest unvisited node to A
   (initially this will be A itself) and call this
   the current node.
   FOR every unvisited node connected to the
   current node:
      Add the distance from the start node to the
      current node to the distance on the edge
      between the current node and the unvisited node.
      If the newly calculated distance is less
      than the shortest recorded distance, then it
      becomes the new shortest recorded distance.
   NEXT connected node
   Mark the current node as visited.
ENDWHILE
```

Example

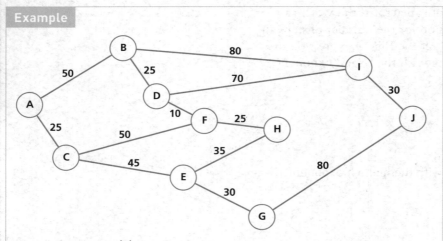

Figure 5.1 **Nodes (1)**

We start by assuming the distance from A to every node is infinity. (From there things can only get better!) The exception to this is A which is a distance of 0 from itself.

We start with the closest node to A (which in this case is A) and mark it as the 'current node'.

Node	Shortest distance from A	Previous node
A (C)	0	
B	∞	
C	∞	
D	∞	
E	∞	
F	∞	
G	∞	
H	∞	
I	∞	
J	∞	

We then calculate the distance to A from all the nodes directly connected to A. If it is shorter than the currently recorded distance then the new distance is recorded and a record is made of the current node in the previous node column so we know how we got to this node.

Node	Shortest distance from A	Previous node
A (C)	0	
B	∞ 50	A
C	∞ 25	A
D	∞	
E	∞	
F	∞	
G	∞	
H	∞	
I	∞	
J	∞	

Now we mark A as visited and repeat the process. C is now the closest unvisited node to A so we look at the nodes directly connected to C, namely F and E.

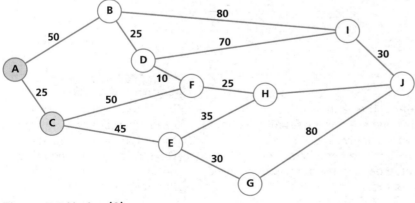

Figure 5.2 **Nodes (2)**

To update E and F, we add the distance of the current node C from A (in this case 25) to the distance from the current node C to the connecting nodes. In our example the distance to F is 75 (that is, 25 + 50) and the distance to E is 70 (that is, 25 + 45).

We only update the values in the table if the values we have calculated are less than the values already in the table. In this case, the values in the table for E and F are infinity so we update them both and put the current node in the 'Previous node' column.

Node	Shortest distance from A	Previous node
A (C)	0	
B	∞ 50	A
C (C)	∞ 25	A
D	∞	
E	∞ 70	C
F	∞ 75	C
G	∞	
H	∞	
I	∞	
J	∞	

B now becomes the current node and the process continues until J has been marked as the current node. We know the shortest distance from A to J is 160. Then, by following the previous nodes from J to A, the route can be determined. The node previous to J is I, previous to I is B and previous to B is A.

Node	Shortest distance from A	Previous node
A (V)	0	
B (V)	∞ 50	A
C (V)	∞ 25	A
D (V)	∞	B
E (V)	∞ 70	C
F (V)	∞ 75	C
G (V)	∞ 100	E
H (V)	∞ 100	EF
I (V)	∞ 130	B
J (C)	∞ 180 160	GI

Exam tip

Two key points to remember in the heat of the exam are:
1 The shortest distance and previous node are only updated *if* the new shortest distance is less than the one already recorded.
2 The algorithm finishes when the destination node is marked as the 'current node'. It may be given a value before this but you only know it is the shortest once it has been visited.

Revision activity

Find out the distances of roads connecting cities in the UK. Pick two and use Dijkstra's algorithm to find out the shortest distance between them.

A* search

Whilst Dijkstra's algorithm always finds the shortest path, it doesn't always go about finding it in the quickest way. A* search is a variation of Dijkstra's that uses a **heuristic** to try and get to the correct solution sooner. The heuristic we use is taking the straight line distance from each node to the destination node.

Heuristic A rule of thumb or estimate.

As before, we start at A and work out the values for B and C. But this time, instead of assigning them the value of the edge, we use the distance from A (which we will call 'g') plus the heuristic value of the distance to J (which we will call 'h'). We will call their sum 'f'.

Node	Path distance (g)	Heuristic distance (h)	f = g+h	Previous node
A	0	95	95	
B	50	80	130	A
C	25	90	115	A
D		75		
E		70		
F		65		
G		50		
H		45		
I		25		
J		0		

We then pick the unvisited node with the lowest value for f and make it the current node (in this case: C).

Node	Path distance (g)	Heuristic distance (h)	f=g+h	Previous node
A	**0**	**95**	**95**	
B	50	80	130	A
C	25	90	115	A
D		75		
E	70	70	140	C
F	75	65	140	C
G		50		
H		45		
I		25		
J		0		

We repeat this until J is the current node. Just like Dijkstra's algorithm we only update when the new value for f is better than the existing one.

Now test yourself

TESTED ☐

5 Describe an advantage of A* search over Dijkstra's algorithm.

Answers on page 149

Topic 2 Problem solving

Exam practice

1 Demonstrate a binary search for the letter E on the following list:

A	B	C	D	E	F	G	H	I	J	K
0	1	2	3	4	5	6	7	8	9	10

[2]

2 Demonstrate a merge sort on the following list:

D	A	B	F	E	C

[3]

3 Demonstrate quicksort on the following list:

C	F	D	E	A	B

[3]

4 An algorithm can take up to $3n^3 - 4n^2 + 6n - 1$ steps to solve a data set n items big.
   (a) Express the algorithm's complexity in Big-O notation. [1]
   (b) State the complexity class of the algorithm. [1]

5 Use Dijkstra's algorithm to work out the shortest path from B to G. [3]

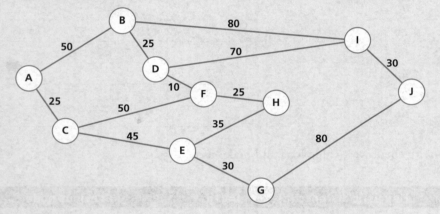

Figure 5.3

Answers on page 160

Summary

- Linear search searches a list one item at a time until the element is found.
- Binary search continually divides a list in two until the element is found.
- Binary search performs better but requires the list to be sorted.
- Bubble sort repeatedly passes through a list, swapping adjacent items.
- Insertion sort takes each item and shuffles it left until it is in order.
- Merge sort splits a list into individual lists one item big. Lists are paired and merged in order. This is repeated until there is one, single, sorted list.

- Quick sort picks an element from the list and creates two sub-lists, bigger and smaller than this element. The same process is reapplied over and over to the sub-lists.
- Complexity of an algorithm shows how well the time it takes scales as the data set it runs on gets bigger.
- Complexities can be constant, linear, polynomial, exponential and logarithmic.
- We can represent the complexity of an algorithm using Big-O notation.
- Dijkstra's algorithm finds the shortest path between two points in a graph.
- A* search improves on Dijkstra's algorithm by using heuristics.

6 Types of programming language

There are many types of programming language. The ones you should understand for the course are **procedural**, **object-oriented** and **assembly**.

> **Procedural programming** Instructions are given in sequence; selection is used to decide what a program does; and iteration dictates how many times it does it. In procedural programming, programs are broken down into key blocks called 'procedures' and 'functions'. Examples of procedural languages include BASIC, C and Pascal.
>
> **Object-oriented programming** A programming style in which a solution consists of objects that interact with each other. Examples of object-oriented languages include Java and C++.
>
> **Assembly language** Mnemonics (memorable letter sequences) are used in place of machine-code instructions. The set of instructions varies from processor to processor, meaning that assembly code written for one processor will not necessarily work on another.

High-level and low-level languages

REVISED

Procedural and object-oriented are examples of high-level language types. A high-level language is one designed to be closer to the way we express ourselves, using a mixture of English words and mathematical expressions. These languages can be converted to machine code.

Low-level languages are those that are directly linked to the architecture of the computer. Machine code and assembly code are low-level languages.

Now test yourself

TESTED

1 Is JavaScript a high- or low-level language? Explain your answer.

Answer on page 150

Assembly language (Little Man Computer)

Machine code uses binary sequences to represent instructions (opcodes) and data on which they act (operands). Rather than having to remember which binary sequence represents which instruction, assembly code allows us to use mnemonics to represent these sequences.

As each assembly code instruction represents a machine code instruction, assembly code programs can often be much longer than their high-level equivalents.

Each processor family has its own assembly language instruction set. In this course you will be using the Little Man Computer instruction set. (The 'Little Man Computer' is a hypothetical machine used to teach the principles of assembly language programming.)

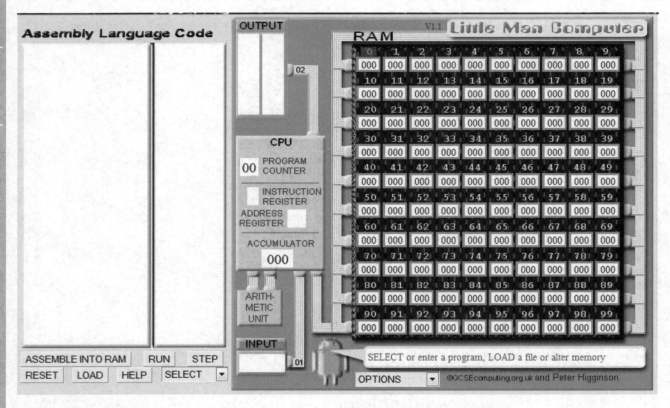

Figure 6.1 Online Little Man Computer simulator (http://peterhigginson.co.uk/LMC)

Little Man Computer uses 11 instructions:

Mnemonic	Instruction
ADD	Add
SUB	Subtract
STA	Stores value from the accumulator to memory
LDA	Loads value from the memory to the accumulator
BRA	Branch always
BRZ	Branch if zero
BRP	Branch if positive
INP	Input
OUT	Output
HLT	End program
DAT	Data location

Now test yourself

TESTED ☐

2 Explain the difference between the BRA, BRZ and BRP instructions.
3 Describe what the LDA instruction does.

Answers on page 150

Each line of an LMC program can have up to four parts: a label, the mnemonic, the data and a comment.

The label is used to identify a line so it can be branched to elsewhere in the program.

```
thisLine ADD 3
```

'thisLine' is a label; the program can jump here with the code.

```
BRA thisLine
```

A label is also used to give a name to a memory location when used with the DAT instruction.

```
attempts DAT 5
```

puts the value 5 in a memory location called 'attempts'.

Example

The following program takes in a number and doubles it.

```
        INP
        STA Num
        ADD Num
        OUT
        HLT
  Num   DAT
```

It works as follows:
1 INP A number is input (and stored in the accumulator): 2
2 STA Num The contents of the accumulator are stored in the memory location labelled Num.
3 ADD Num The contents of Num are added to the accumulator.
4 OUT The contents of the accumulator are output.
5 HLT The program ends.
6 Num DAT A location in memory is labelled Num.

You will notice that the line Num DAT is last but is needed earlier. The memory location Num is allocated when the program is assembled into memory, *before* the program is run.

Now test yourself

TESTED ☐

4 Write an LMC program to triple a number.
5 Write an LMC program that takes in a number and subtracts 1 from it.

Answers on page 150

The branch instructions are used for selection (BRP and BRZ) and iteration (BRA, BRP and BRZ).

Example

Here is an example of selection.

This program outputs 0 if a number less than 10 is entered and 10 if any other number is entered.

```
start       INP
            SUB ten
            BRP tenormore
            LDA zero
            OUT
            BRA end
tenormore   LDA ten
            OUT
end         HLT
ten         DAT 10
zero        DAT 0
```

Now test yourself

TESTED ☐

6 In a high-level language of your choice, write a program equivalent to the one above.
7 Write a program in LMC that takes in a number and trebles it if it is less than 100, otherwise it doubles it.

Answers on page 150

We can perform condition-controlled iteration and count-controlled iteration.

Example

This program demonstrates condition-controlled iteration by asking for a number until one less than 10 is entered:

```
start   INP
        STA num
        SUB ten
        BRP start
        HLT
num     DAT
ten     DAT 10
```

Notice how the BRP instruction is used to loop back round to the start if the number is greater than ten (the result is positive when 10 is subtracted from entered number).

This program demonstrates count-controlled iteration by counting down from a number input to zero.

```
start       INP
takeoneoff  OUT
            SUB one
            BRP takeoneoff
            HLT
one         DAT 1
```

Revision activity

Write a program in a high-level language that checks for syntax errors in an LMC program. It should report invalid instructions, incorrect use of labels and incorrect jumps to non-existent locations.

Now test yourself

TESTED

8 Write an LMC program that keeps asking for a number until one greater than 10 is entered.
9 Write an LMC program that takes in a number and outputs the number 1 that many times.

Answers on page 150

A Level only

Memory addressing

REVISED

There are different ways of accessing memory in low-level languages; we call this addressing. You need to know about four kinds of addressing: **direct**, **indirect**, **indexed** and **immediate**.

Example

Location	Contents
0	43
1	
2	3
3	8
4	6
5	
6	9
7	
8	
9	12
10	
11	54
12	32

Using the memory contents above, LDA 6 loads the following values into the accumulator for each type of addressing:

Addressing mode	Value in accumulator after LDA 6
Direct	9
Indirect	12
Immediate	6
Indexed (5 in the index register)	54

Direct addressing The address given is the location of the data to be used. With direct addressing, LDA 43 means 'load the contents location 43 into the accumulator'. LMC uses direct addressing.

Indirect addressing The address given is the memory location that holds the location of the data. If memory location 43 contains the value 119 then, using indirect addressing, LDA 43 means 'load the contents of location 119 into the accumulator'.

Indexed addressing The value given is added to the value stored in the index register to give the memory location. With index addressing, if the index register contains the value 100 then LDA 43 means 'load the contents of location 143 into the accumulator'.

Immediate addressing The address given is not actually an address but the required value. LDA 43 would mean 'load the value 43 into the accumulator'.

Now test yourself

Location	Contents
0	43
1	
2	3
3	8
4	6
5	
6	9
7	
8	
9	12
10	
11	54
12	32

10 Given the memory shown above, state what is stored in the accumulator after the instruction LDA 4 is carried out under the different addressing modes.

Addressing mode	Value in accumulator after LDA 4
Direct	
Indirect	
Immediate	
Indexed (8 in the index register)	

Answers on page 150

Object-oriented programming

REVISED

Object-oriented programming allows a program to solve problems by programming objects that interact with each other. **Classes** are made to create **objects** which contain **methods** and **attributes**.

Class A template used to define an object. It specifies the methods and attributes an object should have. In the following example, House is the class.

Object An instance of a class. In the following example, myHouse is an object.

Method A subroutine associated with an object. In the following example, changeDoorColour and changeFloors are methods. Additionally, new is a special type of method called a 'constructor'. Constructors define how an object is created.

Attribute Variables contained within and associated to an object. In the following example, doorColour, floors and garden are all attributes.

Example

```
class House
   private doorColour
   private floors
   private garden

   public procedure new(givenDoorColour, givenFloors,
   givenGarden)
      doorColour=givenDoorColour
      floors=givenFloors
      garden=givenGarden
   endProcedure

   public procedure changeFloors(givenFloors)
      if givenFloors>0 then
         floors=givenFloors
      endif
   endProcedure

   public procedure changeDoorColour(givenColour)
      doorColour=givenColour
   endProcedure
endclass


//Main Program
myHouse = new House("Red", 2, true)
```

You will notice in the example that the attributes are private (meaning they cannot be accessed from outside the class, and the methods are public. By the attributes being private they cannot be altered from outside the class in ways we do not want. For example, someone cannot set the number of floors to –1. Instead we allow them to be changed via public methods such as changeFloors. We call this **encapsulation**.

A major feature of OOP is **inheritance**. This is where a class inherits the methods and attributes of a parent class as well as having its own. In the example below, *Bungalow* inherits all the methods and attributes of *House*. It has its own attribute *Porch* and method changePorch. (We will assume in our hypothetical example *only* bungalows have porches!)

> **Encapsulation** Ensuring private attributes can only be amended through public methods. This prevents objects being manipulated in unintended ways.
>
> **Inheritance** The ability for a class to inherit the methods and attributes of a parent class. Its 'child' class can have its own methods and attributes and override methods of its parent class.

Example

```
class Bungalow inherits House
   private porch
   public procedure new(givenDoorColour, givenGarden,
   givenPorch)
      floors=1
      porch=givenPorch
      super.new(givenDoorColour,1, givenGarden)
   endprocedure

   public procedure changePorch(newPorch)
      porch=newPorch
   endprocedure
endclass

myBungalow=new Bungalow("Blue",false, true)
```

We will often want to treat objects of different classes *Houses* and *Bungalows* in the same way. Perhaps we have an array composed of *Houses* and *Bungalows* (maybe even other classes derived from *House* too). If we want to change the door colour of everything inside the array to *Blue* we can do this regardless of which of the classes it is. This is an example of **polymorphism**.

```
for i=0 to 100
    houses[i].changeDoorColour("Blue")
next i
```

> **Polymorphism** Meaning 'many forms', polymorphism is the ability for objects of different classes to be treated in the same way. For example, the same method may be applied to objects of different classes.

Now test yourself

TESTED

11 Describe what is meant by a class and an object.
12 Create a class called *Mansion* that inherits from house. It should have the additional attribute *Fountain* that denotes whether or not it has a fountain. The `changeFloors` method needs to be overridden so no mansion can be given fewer than two floors.

Answers on page 150

A Level only

Exam practice

1 Describe the advantages of a high-level language over a low-level language. [2]
2 Write an LMC program that outputs the numbers 1 to 100. [3]
3 (a) Describe an advantage of direct addressing over indirect addressing. [1]
  (b) Describe an advantage of indirect addressing over direct addressing. [1]
4 A library stock-control system is being developed.
  Describe how inheritance might be used in this program. [2]
5 Explain why encapsulation is considered best practice when using object-oriented programming. [1]
6 Write a class called *Dog*.
  (a) It should have the attribute *Colour*. [1]
  (b) It should have a constructor and the method `changeColour`. [2]
  (c) Use encapsulation to ensure the only colours the dog can be changed to are black, brown, white or grey. [3]

Answers on page 161

Summary

- High-level languages use a mixture of English and mathematical expressions and are machine independent, whereas low-level languages use the instructions available to the processor and therefore only work on machines with that processor architecture.
- An example of a low-level language is assembly language, which consists of mnemonics and the data on which they operate. Little Man Computer (LMC) is an artificial example of an assembly language.
- The LMC instruction INP takes an input and stores it in the accumulator.
- OUT outputs the contents of the accumulator to screen.
- LDA x loads the value from memory location x into the accumulator.
- STA x stores the contents of the accumulator into memory location x.
- ADD x adds the contents of memory location x to the contents of the accumulator and stores the result in the accumulator.
- SUB x subtracts the contents of memory location x from the contents of the accumulator and stores the result in the accumulator.
- BRA y, BRP y and BRZ y jump to the instruction labelled y always, if the accumulator holds a positive number and if the accumulator holds zero, respectively. All three can be used for iteration and BRP and BRZ for selection.
- HLT ends the program.
- y DAT x labels a memory location y and stores x inside it.
- Object-oriented programming is a paradigm that breaks a problem down into a series of objects that interact.
- Classes are templates that define the attributes and methods (subroutines) of these objects.
- Inheritance allows a class to inherit all methods and attributes of a parent class (as well as having its own).
- Encapsulation is the practice of keeping attributes in a class private so they can only be accessed through public methods.
- Polymorphism is the ability to use the same code to process different objects according to their type.

7 Software

Software is the programs that run on a computer. We can categorise software in different ways. One of the most common ways to do this is by function. Types of software include **applications**, **utilities** and **systems software**.

Applications software Software that allows the user to do or make something. It includes word processors, spreadsheet packages and photo-editing suites.

Utilities software A relatively small program that has one purpose, usually concerned with the maintenance of the system. Examples include anti-virus software, disk defragmentation software and backup software.

Systems software The software that runs the hardware. The two main types of systems software are operating systems and utilities.

Now test yourself

TESTED

1 Explain what type of software you would classify a compression program as.
2 Explain what type of software you would classify a desktop publishing package as.

Answers on page 151

Types of operating system

REVISED

Operating systems are an essential piece of software in most modern computer systems, managing the hardware itself and the programs running on it. Examples of operating systems are Windows®, OS X®, Linux®, iOS® and Android®.

An operating system has several roles, to:
● manage the hardware of the system
● manage programs installed and being run
● manage the security of the system
● provide an interface between the user and the computer.

There are different types of operating systems including **multi-tasking**, **multi-user**, **distributed**, **embedded** and **real-time**.

Multi-tasking operating system Can run multiple programs simultaneously.

Multi-user operating system Allows multiple users to use a system and its resources simultaneously. It is the simultaneous aspect that is important. An operating system that allows multiple user accounts but only one person to use the system at a time is not classed as a multi-user operating system.

Distributed operating system Allows multiple computers to work together on a single task.

Embedded operating system Designed to run on embedded systems rather than general-purpose computers. An embedded system is a computer that forms part of a device such as a washing machine, vending machine or car's engine management system.

Real-time operating system Designed to carry out actions within a guaranteed amount of time even when left running for long periods. Usually the expected response time is within a small fraction of a second.

Now test yourself

TESTED

3 State three roles of an operating system.
4 Describe the sort of tasks a multi-tasking operating system might carry out simultaneously on a student's computer.

Answers on page 151

How operating systems work

REVISED

Memory management

One of the key jobs of an operating system is the management of memory. Memory stores the programs and data in use by the system. The operating system needs to ensure that:

- memory is used efficiently – programs that are being used need to be stored in memory without space being wasted
- data in memory is secure – most of the time, programs should not have access to other programs' data.

Storing complete programs as a single block of memory is wasteful as it means that parts of the program not being used are taking up memory and as programs are added and removed space can be used inefficiently. For this reason, items in memory are split up. There are two ways programs and data can be split, **paging** and **segmentation**.

RAM is significantly more expensive that secondary storage. A computer system will often have hundreds of times more secondary storage than RAM. When a system is running low on physical memory (that is, RAM), it is able to use an area of the hard disk as **virtual memory**. Pages are swapped from main memory to virtual memory when not needed and then back to main memory when required. If a computer has to swap pages back and forth too often the computer slows down. We call this disk thrashing.

> **Paging** Where programs are divided physically into equal-sized blocks (typically several kilobytes).
>
> **Segmentation** Where programs are divided logically, split into blocks containing modules or routines.
>
> **Virtual memory** The use of secondary storage as an extension of a computer's physical memory.

Now test yourself

TESTED

5 Describe the purpose of virtual memory.
6 Explain the difference between paging and segmentation.

Answers on page 151

Scheduling

REVISED

An operating system has to ensure that each job and user gets sufficient processing time. It does this through scheduling, which is carried out by a **scheduler**.

A scheduler uses a scheduling algorithm to determine how to share processor time. The scheduling algorithms you need to know are: round robin, first come first served, shortest job first, shortest remaining time and multi-level feedback queues.

- **Round robin** – In round robin scheduling, each process is given a fixed amount of time. If it hasn't finished by the end of that time period, it goes to the back of the queue so the next process in line can have its turn.

> **Scheduler** A program that manages the amount of time different processes have in the CPU.

- **First come first served** – First come first served scheduling is just like queuing in a shop. The first process to arrive is dealt with by the CPU until it is finished; meanwhile, any other processes that come along are queued up waiting for their turn.
- **Shortest job first** – Shortest job first picks the job that will take the shortest time and run it until it finishes. Naturally this algorithm needs to know the time each job will take in advance.
- **Shortest remaining time** – In this algorithm, the scheduler estimates how long each process will take. It then picks the one that will take the least amount of time, and runs that. If a job is added with a shorter remaining time, the scheduler is switched to that one.
- **Multi-level feedback queues** – As the name suggests, a multi-level feedback queue uses a number of queues. Each of these queues has a different priority. The algorithm can move jobs between these queues depending on the jobs' behaviour.

Interrupts

REVISED

The CPU needs to know when a device needs its attention. It does this by sending a signal called an interrupt. An **interrupt** has a priority. Interrupts can only take processor time from tasks of a lower priority. When an interrupt is raised, the **operating system** runs the relevant interrupt service routine.

At the end of each iteration of the fetch–decode–execute cycle, the processor checks to see if there are any interrupts. If there are and they are of a higher priority than the current task, the following steps are carried out:

- The contents of the program counter and the other registers are copied to an area of memory called a stack.
- The relevant interrupt service routine can then be loaded by changing the program counter to the value of where the ISR starts in memory.
- When the interrupt service routine is complete, the previous values of the program counter and other registers can be restored from memory to the CPU.

If, while an interrupt is being serviced, a new, higher priority interrupt is raised, the interrupt currently being serviced is added to a stack in memory and the new interrupt is serviced. Once this new interrupt is finished the previous interrupt is taken off the stack and continued.

> **Interrupt** A signal sent to the processor requesting the processor's attention for a particular event.
>
> **Operating system** The software that manages a computer and its resources.

Now test yourself

TESTED

7 Describe the first come first served scheduling algorithm.
8 Explain the significance of an interrupt having a priority.

Answers on page 151

Device drivers

REVISED

Operating systems are expected to communicate with a wide variety of devices, each with different models and manufacturers. It would be impossible for the makers of operating systems to program them to handle all existing and future devices. This is why we need **device drivers**. A device driver is a piece of software, usually supplied with a device, that tells the operating system how it can communicate with the device.

> **Device driver** A piece of software, usually supplied with a device, that tells the operating system how it can communicate with the device.

BIOS

REVISED

BIOS stands for 'basic input/output system'. When a computer is first switched on it looks to the BIOS to get it up and running, and so the processor's program counter points to the BIOS's memory. The BIOS is usually stored on flash memory so that it can be updated. This also allows settings such as boot order of disks to be changed and saved by the user.

Virtual machines

REVISED

It is possible to write a program that has the same functionality as a physical computer. We call such programs **virtual machines**. They have the advantage that they can be backed up and duplicated and more than one can be run at one time on a physical machine.

> **Virtual machine** A program that has the same functionality as a physical computer.

A common use of virtual machines is to run operating systems within another operating system. This might be because a program is needed that will not run on the host operating system or it might be because it offers a convenient way to test a program being developed on multiple platforms.

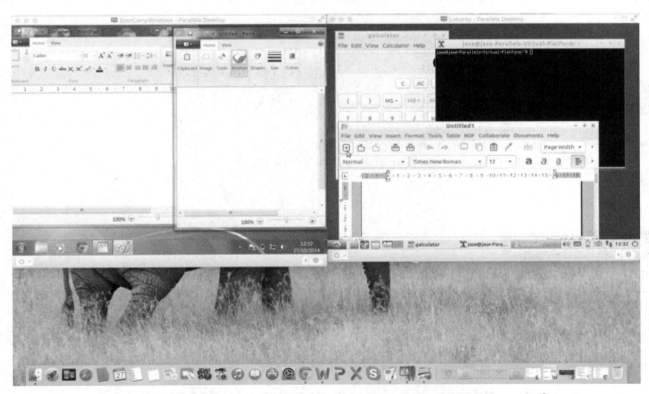

Figure 7.1 Windows 7® and Lubuntu Linux® running in virtual machines in OS X Yosemite®

Another common use of virtual machines is interpreting intermediate code. A compiler converts the source code into something called byte code. This isn't machine code but is a much more efficient representation than the original source code. Because it is not machine code it cannot be run directly on a processor. Instead, a virtual machine is used to read the code. Any device running this virtual machine can read this intermediate code making it highly portable.

> **Revision activity**
>
> Install VirtualBox, a free virtual machine, and experiment with using different versions of Linux.

Open and closed source software

When software is sold commercially it is compiled to machine code. This means users can run it without having to translate it. Most users would have no need for the program's source code. It would not be wise for the company making the software to supply it as it would mean users could amend their software and steal their work.

Software where the source code is made publicly available is called **open source software** (OSS). This means that users can modify software to suit their needs. It also means that anyone can have a part in the development of software. Examples of OSS are Linux® and OpenOffice™.

Conversely software which is only distributed as executable code is referred to as closed source software. There are advantages and disadvantages of each:

- Open source software is free.
- Users are free to amend the source code of open source software.
- Closed source software is developed by companies with lots of resources and teams of programmers working at the same location. They often (but not always) tend to be more polished.
- Open source software is developed sometimes by huge teams of volunteers across the world who are not constrained by the commercial considerations of the project.
- Open source software has the advantage that anyone can help find security holes in it but this also includes those who may exploit such failures maliciously before they are fixed.

> **Open source software**
> Software that has its source code freely available and grants users the right to examine, modify and share it.

Now test yourself

9 Describe what is meant by a device driver.
10 Explain an advantage and disadvantage of distributing a program as byte code (intermediate code) to be run on a virtual machine.

Answers on page 151

Exam practice

1 Describe what is meant by a utility. [1]
2 Explain how an operating system deals with physical memory being full. [2]
3 Explain what happens when an interrupt is generated. [4]
4 Explain a disadvantage of the shortest-job-first scheduling algorithm. [2]
5 Describe a disadvantage of running a program on an operating system on a virtual machine rather than directly off an operating system running off a physical machine. [2]
6 Explain why a company might choose to use closed-source software. [2]

Answers on page 162

Summary

- Applications are programs that allow the user to do or make something.
- Utilities are small programs often used for the upkeep of a system.
- Systems software runs the hardware.
- Operating systems manage system hardware, manage programs being installed or run, provide an interface for the user and manage security.
- One of the jobs of an OS is memory management. Memory can be split logically into segments or physically into pages. When physical memory is full, pages are stored in virtual memory on a secondary storage device.
- Scheduling is used to ensure all jobs get processor time. Scheduling algorithms include: round robin, first come first served, shortest job first, shortest remaining time, multi-level feedback queues.
- Interrupts are used to get the processor to attend to something rather than its current task. An interrupt can only take over from a lower priority process.
- A device driver is a program that allows the operating system to control hardware devices.
- The BIOS is used to help boot the system.
- Virtual machines are programs that perform the function of a physical computer. Two of the main uses are to run an operating system inside another and to run intermediate code.

8 Applications generation

Translators

REVISED

Computers follow instructions that comprise of an opcode (the instruction itself) and an operand (the data it acts on). We call this machine code. While computers only understand machine code, humans write programs in much easier-to-read programming languages. In order to convert these programming languages to machine code, computers use translator programs.

Assembly code and assemblers

REVISED

Machine code, being made up of just 1s and 0s is very difficult for humans to follow. To get round this, computer scientists started to use assembly code. In assembly code the opcode is represented by a mnemonic (a memorable group of letters) and the operand is represented in denary or hexadecimal. A program called an assembler is then used to convert each line of assembly code into machine code.

Interpreters and compilers

REVISED

Writing assembly code is laborious; many lines of code are needed for the simplest of tasks. Fortunately high-level languages were invented. A high-level language is one that consists of more easily human-readable statements. Over time, many high-level languages have been created including (to name just a few) BASIC, C, C++, JavaScript® and Python®.

For a computer to run a program written in a high-level language it needs to be converted to machine code. To do this we can use a **compiler** or an **interpreter**.

A compiler takes code written in a high-level language and builds an executable machine code program.

An interpreter takes each line of a high-level language program, converts it to machine code and runs it before reading the next line.

A compiler can take a while to do the translation but once the executable is built it can be run immediately. An interpreter can start running the program straight away but it will run slower than it would if compiled as the interpreter has to translate each line as it is run.

Interpreters can be useful during the coding and debugging process as the programmer does not have to wait for compilation and will stop at a line if it finds an error. On the other hand, when distributing a program, a compiled version is better: it runs quicker, does not require any additional software to run and is harder to change (than it would be if the source code was available).

> **Compiler** A translator program that converts high-level source code into an executable machine-code file.
>
> **Interpreter** A translator program that reads and executes a program line by line.

Now test yourself

TESTED

1 Explain why a programmer might use an interpreter rather than a compiler.
2 Describe what is meant by a high-level language.

Answers on page 151

How a compiler works

Compilers generally work by going through the following steps: lexical analysis, syntax analysis, code generation and optimisation.

Lexical analysis

During lexical analysis:

- comments and whitespace are removed from the program
- the remaining code is turned into a series of tokens (specific sequences of characters)
- a symbol table is created to keep track of the variables and subroutines (this includes information such as data type and scope).

Syntax analysis

Syntax is the structure of a language. Computer languages, just like spoken languages, have a specific structure (for example, you would usually be able to write a = b+c but not b+c = a).

In syntax analysis:

- an abstract syntax tree is built from the tokens produced during lexical analysis
- if any tokens break the rules of the language, syntax errors are generated.

Code generation

During code generation the abstract code tree is converted to object code. Object code is machine code before the final step (the linker) is run.

Code optimisation

Optimisation tweaks the code so it will run as quickly as possible (or sometimes using as little memory as possible).

Now test yourself

TESTED

3 List the stages of compilation.
4 Describe what is stored in the symbol table.

Answers on page 151

Libraries

REVISED

Often code to perform complex tasks has already been written (and usually compiled) and packaged as a **library**. This code can be reused by other programmers.

Libraries have the advantages that:

- they save time, rather than rewriting code someone else has written
- they can cover complex areas that require expertise in an area and would be time consuming to code
- a library coded in one language can be used in programs written in another language.

> **Library** A pre-written collection of code that allows programmers to import functionality into their own programs.

Linkers and loaders

A linker is used to combine compiled code with that from a library into a single executable file.

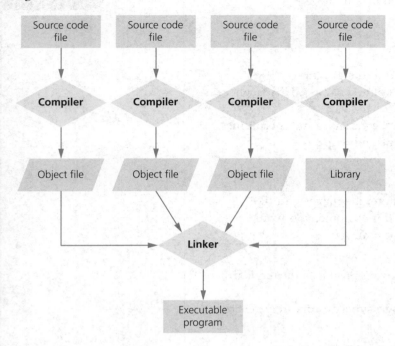

A loader is part of the operating system and is responsible for loading a program into memory.

Now test yourself

TESTED

5 Explain why programmers use libraries.
6 State the purpose of a linker.

Answers on page 151

A Level only

Exam practice

1 Explain the similarities and differences between a compiler and an assembler. [2]
2 Explain why programmers might use an interpreter. [2]
3 Describe what happens in the lexical analysis stage of compilation. [2]
4 State what a loader does. [1]

Answers on page 162

Summary

- Compilers, interpreters and assemblers are all types of translator program.
- A compiler converts code in a high-level language into machine code.
- An interpreter converts and runs high-level code line by line.
- An assembler converts low-level assembly code into machine code.

- Compilers work through the stages: lexical analysis, syntax analysis, code generation and optimisation.
- Libraries are pre-written bodies of code that can be used by programmers.
- Linkers combine different pieces of compiled code, including that from libraries, into a single executable compiled code.
- Loaders load a program into memory.

9 Software development

Building large pieces of software is an expensive and time-consuming process with plenty of scope for projects to run over time and budget or even fail completely. Methodologies have been developed to help ensure the success of software projects.

Elements of software development

REVISED

Feasibility study

The purpose of a **feasibility study** is to determine if a project is likely to be successful. There are a number of reasons a project might fail, including:
- the budget may not be big enough or the cost of the project too high compared to the benefits – in other words, the project may not be economically feasible
- it might be that the project would break laws about data protection and privacy – it might not be legally feasible
- there may not be enough time for the project to be realistically completed
- the project could be overly ambitious and go beyond what current hardware or algorithms can achieve – it might not be technically feasible.

For these reasons, the first step of any project should be a feasibility study so that any issues that make a project unviable can be addressed and, if necessary, the project can be set aside until such a time as it becomes possible.

> **Feasibility study** The initial investigation that determines whether a project is viable before time and resources are invested in it.

Requirements specification

A **requirements specification** document is the agreement between client and developer as to exactly what the system should be able to do.
- The requirements are acquired through a process known as requirements elicitation. This may involve interviews, observations, questionnaires, and so on.
- The requirements specification can act as a contract and will often form the basis of the acceptance testing.

> **Requirements specification** A document listing all the functionality the system should have.

Testing

Testing ensures the system works as it should. The programmers will test the system continually throughout the coding process. There are a number of other forms of testing that should take place throughout the project: **destructive**, **alpha**, **beta** and **acceptance testing**.

> **Revision activity**
>
> Pick your favourite computer game. Write a requirements specification that could have been used for this game.

> **Destructive testing** Testers try to cause a program to crash or behave unexpectedly.
>
> **Alpha testing** Where the product is used within the development company by people who have not worked on the project.
>
> **Beta testing** A small group of users from outside the software company use the software to see if they encounter any bugs or usability problems not picked up during the previous testing.
>
> **Acceptance testing** When the user tests the program against every requirement in the requirements specification. Once this testing is successful, the project can be signed off.

Documentation

A number of written documents are produced during the software engineering process:

- **Requirements specification** – detailing exactly what the system should be able to do.
- **Design** – might include algorithms, screen layout designs and descriptions of how data will be stored.
- **Technical documentation** – details how the system works so it can be maintained in future. This may include descriptions of the code, its modules and their functionality.
- **User documentation** – tells the user how to operate the system. This may include tutorials on how to use the system, descriptions of error messages and a troubleshooting guide about how to overcome common problems.

Now test yourself

TESTED

1 Describe what is checked during a feasibility study.
2 Explain what is meant by alpha testing.
3 Describe what is meant by user documentation.

Answers on page 152

Methodologies

REVISED

To ensure software projects are delivered on time and on budget, different methodologies have been developed.

Waterfall lifecycle

The waterfall lifecycle is a well-known and often criticised development model.

- The waterfall lifecycle consists of a sequence of stages; each stage is started only after the previous one is complete.
- It is possible to go back a stage when necessary.
- Exact stages can vary but usually are: requirements definition, analysis, design, coding, testing, maintenance.
- It works well where there is a clear expected output at each stage and everyone has clear responsibilities.
- It is not suited to high risk projects. If a problem is discovered at a later stage a lot of work (and therefore time and money) may have been wasted.

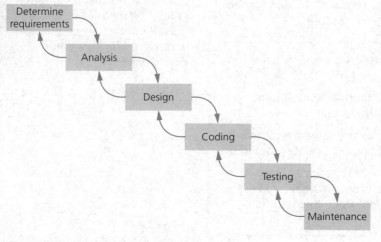

Figure 9.1 The waterfall lifecycle

Rapid application development

Rapid application development (RAD) involves the use of prototypes. (A prototype is a version of the system that lacks full functionality.)

- The user is shown the prototype and gives feedback that is used to inform how the prototype is further developed.
- This continues until the end user is happy that the prototype has all the required functionality. At this point it becomes the end product.
- Rapid application development is well suited to projects where the requirements aren't entirely clear from the outset.
- With continuous feedback from the client, the end product is likely to have excellent usability though the code may not be particularly efficient.
- It is necessary to have frequent contact with the end user.
- It does not scale well and so is less suited to large projects with big teams.

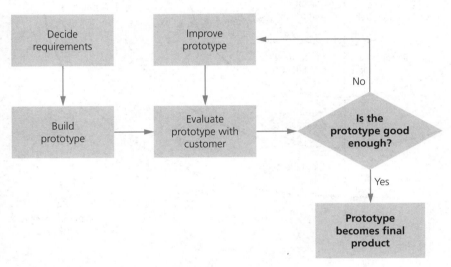

Figure 9.2 **Rapid application development**

Spiral model

The spiral model is designed to try and manage risk. It consists of four stages, each forming a quadrant of the spiral that are iterated through:

1 **Determine objectives** – The first stage is to determine the objectives of that rotation of the spiral according to the biggest potential risks.
2 **Identify and resolve risks** – In the next stage, the possible risks are identified and alternative options considered. If risks are considered too high at this stage, the project may be stopped.
3 **Development and testing** – The third stage allows the part of the project being worked on to be made and tested.
4 **Plan next iteration** – The fourth stage determines what will happen in the next iteration of the spiral.

The spiral cycle manages risk well but requires practitioners skilled in risk management.

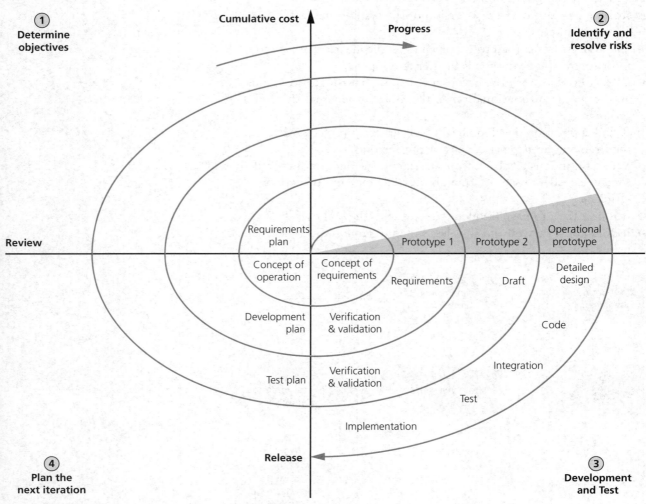

Figure 9.3 **The spiral model**

Agile software development

Agile software development is not a single methodology but a group of methods. These methods are designed to cope with changing requirements through producing the software in an iterative manner; that is to say, it is produced in versions, each building on the previous one and each increasing the requirements it meets.

Extreme programming

An example of an agile software development methodology is extreme programming (often abbreviated to XP); a methodology that puts the emphasis on the coding itself.

- A representative of the customer becomes part of the team to help decide the 'user stories' (XP's equivalent of requirements and how these will be tested) and to answer questions.
- XP is iterative in nature (the program is coded, tested and improved repeatedly), using shorter (week long) iterations than RAD.
- Each iteration in XP produces a version of the system (albeit lacking some of the requirements) with code of a good enough quality to be used in the final product.

- XP uses pair programming. This is when code is written with two programmers sitting next to each other, one writing the code and the other analysing what is being written, and then switching roles at regular intervals.
- Programmers are encouraged to regularly 'refactor' code; that is, make it more efficient without changing what it does.
- Every programmer is responsible for the entire program.
- With such an emphasis on programming, the quality of the final code is likely to be very high.
- The client needs to be able to commit to having a representative working with the team.

Now test yourself

TESTED

4 Describe the purpose of the prototype in rapid application development.
5 List the stages of the waterfall lifecycle model.
6 Describe the spiral model.

Answers on page 152

Exam practice

1 Describe the risks of failing to carry out a feasibility study. [2]
2 Explain why beta testing is important. [2]
3 Explain the purpose of technical documentation. [2]
4 Explain how extreme programming is likely to lead to high-quality code. [3]
5 Explain why the spiral model would be a better choice than the waterfall lifecycle model for a high-risk project. [4]

Answers on page 163

Summary

- A feasibility study determines whether a project is likely to be successful before it is started.
- A requirements specification is a document that records all the proposed functionality of a system.
- Testing seeks to identify problems in a system.
- The waterfall lifecycle involves one stage being completed after another. A stage is only started when the previous one is complete.
- In rapid application development a prototype is produced. The user evaluates it and the feedback is used to improve it. This process is continued until a final product is produced.

- The spiral model takes an iterative approach centred around risk. The biggest risks are identified and resolved in each iteration.
- Agile software development is a set of methodologies that work well with potentially changing requirements. One of these methodologies is extreme programming.
- Extreme programming uses techniques such as pair programming and refactoring to produce high-quality code. A representative of the user works with the development team throughout the process.

10 Computer systems

Hardware is the description given to the physical components of a computer system.

A computer system has a central processing unit and memory. There is usually some form of storage and devices to input data into and output information from the computer. A peripheral is the term given to devices external to the processor. Peripherals are either input, output or storage devices.

Input, output and storage

REVISED

Input devices allow data to be entered into a computer. Examples include keyboards, mice, microphones, scanners and joysticks.

Output devices allow information to be retrieved from a computer. Examples include printers, speakers, monitors and actuators (devices that cause movement).

Storage devices fall into three categories: magnetic, flash and optical:

1 **Magnetic storage** – uses a magnetisable material. Patterns of magnetisation are then used to represent binary sequences. Examples include hard disk drives and magnetic tape (often used to back up servers). Magnetic storage tends to have a high capacity at a low cost.

2 **Optical storage** – such as CDs, DVDs and Blu-ray discs™ work by using a laser and by looking at its reflection, determining where there are pits on a surface representing 1s and 0s. Optical media tend to be cheap to distribute and fairly resilient.

3 **Flash media** – work by using a special type of ROM that can be overwritten. Flash memory is used in USB memory sticks, camera memory cards and solid state drives. Whilst expensive, it can be read from and written to at high speeds and as it has no moving parts, has lower power consumption and is unaffected by sudden movements.

> **Input device** A device that allows data to be entered into a computer system.
>
> **Output device** A device that allows information to be received from a computer system.

Now test yourself

TESTED

1 List ten different input devices.
2 List ten different output devices.
3 Find out and describe the storage devices your school or college uses to store and back up students' data.

Answers on page 152

The central processing unit (CPU)

REVISED

The **central processing unit (CPU)** carries out the instructions in computer programs. Inside a processor there are billions of transistors (effectively electronic switches).

Processors work at incredible speeds, dictated by the clock signal. The speed of this signal or clock speed is measured in hertz.

> **Central processing unit (CPU)** The processor that carries out the instructions in computer programs.

Unit	Pulses per second
1 Hertz	1
1 Kilohertz	1000
1 Megahertz	1000000
1 Gigahertz	1000000000

Modern desktop processors tend run in the order of Gigahertz.

Clock speed is not the only aspect of a processor that affects its performance. Other factors include:
- cache memory
- multiple cores
- pipelining.

Cache memory

RAM is significantly slower than the speed at which the CPU operates. To compensate for this, processors have a small amount of fast memory called **cache**. Cache memory is built into the processor itself, reducing the distance data has to travel to it. By anticipating the data and instructions that are likely to be regularly accessed and keeping these in cache memory, the overall speed at which the processor operates is less likely to be limited by the speed of the RAM.

> **Cache** A temporary store where instructions or data that are likely to be needed are anticipated and are stored, ready for fast access.

Multiple cores

Each core is a distinct processing unit on the CPU. As well as having their own cache, the cores will also share a higher-level cache. When multi-tasking, different cores can run different applications. It is also possible for multiple cores to work on the same problem.

> **A Level only**

Pipelining

The processor works by repeatedly fetching, decoding and executing instructions. If it does this one at a time, then parts of the processor are potentially left sitting idle. Pipelining means that as an instruction is being decoded, the one after that can be fetched.

	Fetch	Decode	Execute
Step 1	Instruction 1		
Step 2	Instruction 2	Instruction 1	
Step 3	Instruction 3	Instruction 2	Instruction 1
Step 4	Instruction 4	Instruction 3	Instruction 2

This works as long as subsequent instructions can be predicted. If the wrong instruction is chosen to be fetched in advance it has to be thrown away and the correct one fetched.

Inside the processor

Registers

Registers are areas of memory within the processor itself. They work at extremely fast speeds so can be used by the processor without causing a bottleneck.

The registers you need to know of are:
- **Program counter (PC)** – keeps track of the memory location of the line of machine code being executed. With each iteration of the fetch–decode–execute cycle it gets incremented to point to the next instruction, allowing the program to be executed in sequence, one by one. The program counter can also be changed by instructions that alter the flow of control (for example, branch like BRA, BRP and BRZ).

- **Memory data register (MDR)** – stores the data that has been fetched from or stored in memory.
- **Memory address register (MAR)** – stores the address of the data or instructions that are to be fetched from or sent to.
- **Current instruction register (CIR)** – stores the most recently fetched instruction, waiting to be decoded and executed.
- **Accumulator (ACC)** – stores the results of calculations made by the **arithmetic logic unit (ALU)**.
- **General purpose registers** – Processors may also have general purpose registers. These can be used temporarily to store data being used rather than sending data to and from the comparatively much slower memory.
- **Buses** – are the communication channels through which data can be sent around the computer. You need to know about three buses:
  1 The data bus carries data between the processor and memory.
  2 The address bus carries the address of the memory location being read from or written to.
  3 The control bus sends control signals from the **control unit**.

> **Arithmetic logic unit (ALU)** Carries out the calculations and logical decisions. The results of its calculations are stored in the accumulator.
>
> **Control unit (CU)** Sends out signals to co-ordinate how the processor works. It controls how data moves around parts of the CPU and how it moves between the CPU and memory. Instructions are decoded in the control unit.

> **Exam tip**
>
> A common mistake is to talk about the control bus carrying instructions around the processor. This is not the case. Instructions are sent to and from memory via the data bus. The control bus carries the signals orchestrating the fetch–decode–execute signal.

How the fetch–decode–execute cycle affects the registers

REVISED

The processor works by continually fetching, decoding then executing instructions. You need to be aware of how the registers are used during the process.

Fetch

1 The PC is copied to the MAR.
2 The fetch signal is sent across the control bus, the contents of the MAR across the address bus.
3 The contents of the memory location stored in the MAR are then sent across the data bus and stored in the CIR.
4 The PC is incremented by one.

Decode

5 The contents of the CIR are sent to the control unit.
6 The control unit then decodes the instruction.

Execute

7 The registers can be changed in different ways during the execution phase, depending on the instruction.
  If a memory location is to be read from or written to (that is, LDA or STA) then the address stored within the instruction will be loaded into the MAR. In the case of STA the data is stored in the ACC and sent to memory, in the case of memory it is loaded from memory into the ACC. If the instruction is to carry out a calculation (that is, ADD or SUB) then the contents of the MDR and ACC are sent to the ALU and the result sent back to the ACC.

Memory: RAM and ROM

There are two forms of primary memory (that is, memory the CPU can access directly): **RAM (Random Access Memory)** and ROM (Read Only Memory).

> **RAM (Random Access Memory)** The primary memory that stores the programs and data the system is currently using.

RAM:

1 Stores the parts of the operating system, programs in use.
2 Is volatile (that is, loses its contents when power is lost).
3 Can have any location read from or written to at equal speed to any other location.

ROM:

1 Is non-volatile (that is, retains its contents when power is lost).
2 Is read-only and so cannot be written to.
3 Is often used to store the computer's boot program.

Now test yourself

TESTED

4 Describe the purpose of the control unit.
5 Give an example of when the contents of the ACC might be changed.
6 State one difference between RAM and ROM.

Answers on page 152

A Level only

Graphics processing unit (GPU)

REVISED

A **graphics processing unit (GPU)** is specifically designed to perform the calculations associated with graphics. GPUs:
- have **instruction sets** specifically designed for the sorts of calculations required in graphics processing
- have the ability to process these pieces of data in parallel; what is referred to as single instruction multiple data (SIMD)
- can be placed on a graphics card with access to their own dedicated memory
- can be embedded onto a CPU.

> **Graphics processing unit** A specialised processor designed for processing data for graphics but now being applied in other fields too.
>
> **Instruction sets** The complete set of instructions that can be recognised and executed by the processor.

Whilst designed for graphics (for example for gaming animation and design), GPUs are increasingly being used in many other fields. Examples include:
- modelling physical systems
- audio processing
- breaking passwords
- machine learning.

Computer architectures

Von Neumann and Harvard architectures

You need to understand what is meant by the Von Neumann and Harvard architectures.

The **Von Neumann architecture**:
- has a single control unit
- works sequentially through instructions
- stores instructions and data together in the same memory unit.

The Harvard architecture differs in that it has separate memory units for data and instructions.

> **Von Neumann architecture**
> An architecture that has a single control unit, processes instructions in a linear fashion and stores data and instructions in the same memory unit.

Parallel processing

Parallel processing is when a computer carries out multiple computations simultaneously to solve a given problem. There are different approaches to this:
- One is single instruction multiple data (SIMD), where the same operation is carried out on multiple pieces of data, at one time. This type of parallel processing is often carried out by GPUs.
- The other approach is multiple instructions multiple data (MIMD); here, different instructions are carried out concurrently on different pieces of data. This could, on one hand, be carried out using multiple cores on a CPU or, to the other extreme, be executed across super computers with thousands of CPUs.

There is a limit as to how much more quickly parallel processing can solve a problem, depending on how much of the problem is parallelisable.

RISC vs CISC

There are two main approaches to CPUs – **RISC (Reduced Instruction Set Computing)** and **CISC (Complex Instruction Set Computing)**.
- RISC processors have a smaller range of instructions than CISC processors.
- The smaller instruction set means fewer transistors are needed meaning they generally require less power and cost less to produce.
- The instructions in a CISC processor may take several clock cycles to execute. RISC instructions usually take a single clock cycle meaning pipelining can be used.
- Compilers for RISC processors tend to be more complicated so for a given program more instructions are likely to be generated.
- RISC processors have fewer addressing modes than CISC processors but more general-purpose registers.

> **RISC (reduced instruction set computing)** Processors with a limited instruction set. Instructions execute in a single clock cycle, allowing pipelining.
>
> **CISC (complex instruction set computing)** Non-RISC processors.

Now test yourself

7 Explain what is meant by MIMD.
8 Explain what is meant by SIMD.
9 State which has more addressing modes: a CISC or a RISC processor.

Answers on page 152

Exam practice

1 Explain why smartphones use flash memory. [2]
2 Describe the purpose of the address bus. [1]
3 Give two differences between RISC and CISC processors. [2]
4 Describe the Von Neumann architecture. [2]
5 Explain what is meant by a GPU. [2]

Answers on page 163

Summary

- Input devices allow data to be entered into a computer; output devices allow computers to give out information.
- Storage devices can use magnetic, optical or flash storage.
- The central processing unit (CPU) carries out the instructions in programs. The faster the clock speed (measured in GHz), the more instructions it can execute per second.
- Processor performance can be improved by increasing the number of cores, increasing the amount of cache memory or using pipelining.
- Random Access Memory is volatile and stores the programs and data in use.
- Read Only Memory is non-volatile and is often used to store the computer's boot program.

- A graphics processing unit (GPU) is a specialist processor for rendering 3D graphics.
- The Von Neumann architecture follows the fetch–decode–execute cycle and uses one ALU and one control unit. Programs and data are stored together in memory.
- In the Harvard architecture, programs and data are stored in separate memory units.
- Parallel processing is the processing of multiple pieces of data at the same time. This could be with the same instruction being applied to all the data (SIMD) or different instructions (MIMD).
- RISC is an alternative processor architecture, which has a reduced instruction set. These instructions require fewer clock cycles to execute and mean the processor requires fewer transistors to build.

11 Data types

Why we need data types

REVISED

Whatever the data type is, it is stored in the computer in **binary**.

When we look at data, we instinctively recognise the type of data from our experience; a computer is not able to do this. Different data types are stored and processed in different ways, which means we have to tell the computer what type data it is so that appropriate facilities for processing and storing are made available.

> **Binary** Number system with a base of 2.

Data types

REVISED

The main data types we use are:

Type	Description	Example
Character	Single letter, digit, symbol or control code	S, g, 7, &
String	A string of alphanumeric characters	hat, Fg7tY6, %7&*j
Boolean	One of two values	True or False
Integer	Whole number values with no decimal part	6, –12, 9, 143
Real	Numbers with decimal or fractional parts	12.3, –18.63, 3.14

Representing data

REVISED

Text

One approach to representing data is ASCII:
- Each character of the alphabet and some special symbols and control codes are represented by agreed binary patterns.
- The ASCII character set was originally based on an 8-bit binary pattern using seven bits plus a single parity bit and was able to represent 128 separate characters.
- The extended ASCII set uses eight bits and so can represent 256 separate characters.
- With just eight bits available in the ASCII system the number of characters is limited to 256, making it impossible to display the wide range of characters for other alphabets or symbols sets.

Another approach is Unicode:
- Unicode was originally a 16-bit code allowing for more than 65 000 characters to be represented.
- This was updated to remove the 16-bit restriction by using a series of code pages with each page representing the chosen language symbols.
- The original ASCII representations have been included as part of the Unicode character set with the same numeric values.

A string is simply a collection of characters and uses as many bytes as required, so if using the ASCII 8-bit character set, the string 'HODDER' would require one byte per character, or six bytes, to store the string.

Boolean data

Boolean is a data type that can only take one of two values: TRUE or FALSE, using 1 to represent TRUE and 0 to represent FALSE.

- Boolean data only requires one bit to store a value.
- Boolean data types are often used to flag if an event has occurred.

Integers

Positive integers in binary

When we write a number in base 2, binary, we use a similar approach to writing numbers in base 10, but the column headings are based on 2 rather than 10.

The conversion from binary to **denary** is straightforward: add the column values together for every column containing a 1 in the binary number.

> **Denary** Number system with a base of 10.

Example

Column value	$128=2^7$	$64=2^6$	$32=2^5$	$16=2^4$	$8=2^3$	$4=2^2$	$2=2^1$	$1=2^0$
Binary number	1	0	0	1	0	1	1	0
In base 10	128+	0+	0+	16+	0+	4+	2+	0

128+16+4+2=150 in base 10 (denary).

Converting denary numbers to binary can be done by dividing repeatedly by 2 and recording the remainder until we reach 0.

Example

155 in denary into binary is:

$155 \div 2 = 77$ remainder 1 (the number of 1s)

$77 \div 2 = 38$ remainder 1 (the number of 2s)

$38 \div 2 = 19$ remainder 0

$19 \div 2 = 9$ remainder 1 (the number of 8s)

$9 \div 2 = 4$ remainder 1 (the number of 16s)

$4 \div 2 = 2$ remainder 0

$2 \div 2 = 1$ remainder 0

$1 \div 2 = 0$ remainder 1 (the number of 128s)

So 155 in binary is 10011011

Check: 128+16+8+2+1 = 155 ✓

Now test yourself

TESTED ☐

1 Convert the following binary numbers to denary:
   (a) 10000010
   (b) 11000001
   (c) 11011000
2 Convert the following denary numbers to 8-bit binary values:
   (a) 140
   (b) 68
   (c) 200

Answers on page 153

> **Exam tip**
>
> With practice, these conversions can be done in your head but you should *always* double check your answer.

Negative integers in binary

There are two ways to represent negative integers in binary.

Sign and magnitude

We can follow the convention used in denary and store a sign bit, a + or −, as part of the number.

- We use the left-hand bit, the one with the largest value, often called the **most significant bit (MSB)** to store these as a binary value; 0 for + and 1 for −.

> **Most significant bit (MSB)**
> The bit with the largest value in a multiple-bit binary number.

This modifies the column headings to:

Column value	Sign bit	64	32	16	8	4	2	1

Example

So to store −37 we will need to set the sign bit to 1 and set the remaining columns to store the magnitude, 37.

Column value	Sign bit	64	32	16	8	4	2	1
Binary number	1	0	1	0	0	1	0	1

To store +45 in sign and magnitude representation, we set the sign bit to 0 and the remaining seven bits for the magnitude to 45:

Column value	Sign bit	64	32	16	8	4	2	1
Binary number	0	0	1	0	1	1	0	1

Two's complement

While we humans are quite happy to deal with a sign and a magnitude, the processing required to handle this is quite complicated and a more effective approach is two's complement.

- With two's complement we make the most significant bit (MSB) a negative value.

This changes the column headings for 8-bit numbers to:

Column value	−128	64	32	16	8	4	2	1

Example

To store −88 we record −128 + 40 or:

Column value	−128	64	32	16	8	4	2	1
Binary number	1	0	1	0	1	0	0	0

Check −128 + 32 + 8 = −88 ✓

Now test yourself

3 Convert the following denary numbers to 8-bit two's complement binary values:
   (a) 56
   (b) −72
   (c) −3
4 Convert the following two's complement 8-bit binary values to denary:
   (a) 00101000
   (b) 10111100
   (c) 11001111

Answers on page 153

Hexadecimal

Hexadecimal is a number system based on 16 that is commonly used by programmers working with low-level code or with codes for various types of data, for example when coding in HTML the code for the colour orange is FFA500.

- Computers do not work in hexadecimal (base 16) but it provides a shorthand for those who work in binary that is simpler to understand and remember.
- For example, it is hard to remember and easy to make a mistake entering 11001110001110001101 while the hexadecimal equivalent, CE38D, is much easier to remember and less likely to be entered incorrectly.
- Hexadecimal is convenient because the base, $16 = 2^4$, uses four bits, making direct conversion between binary and hexadecimal possible.
- Hexadecimal is based on 16 and we therefore need 16 symbols to represent the possible values in each column. We use 0–9 for the first ten, then A, B, C, D, E and F to represent 10, 11, 12, 13, 14 and 15.

> **Hexadecimal** Number system with a base of 16.

Denary	Binary	Hexadecimal		Denary	Binary	Hexadecimal
0	0000	0		8	1000	8
1	0001	1		9	1001	9
2	0010	2		10	1010	A
3	0011	3		11	1011	B
4	0100	4		12	1100	C
5	0101	5		13	1101	D
6	0110	6		14	1110	E
7	0111	7		15	1111	F

Converting between binary and hexadecimal simply requires each group of four bits to be replaced by the equivalent hexadecimal symbol.

Converting from hexadecimal to binary, each symbol is replaced by the corresponding group of four bits.

Example

A5D in hexadecimal is 1010 0101 1101 in binary.

Converting between hexadecimal and denary uses column values.

For example, A5D in denary is:

Column value	$16^2=256$	$16^1=16$	$16^0=1$
	A=10	5	D=13

$10 \times 256 + 5 \times 16 + 13 \times 1 = 2653$

Converting from binary to hexadecimal requires repeated division by 16 and noting any remainders.

Example

1461 into hexadecimal:

1461 ÷ 16 = 91 remainder 5 (the number of 1s)

91 ÷ 16 = 5 remainder 11 or B in hexadecimal (the number of 16s)

5 ÷ 16 = 0 remainder 5 (the number of 256s)

1461 is 5B5 in hexadecimal.

Exam tip

When answering questions involving a calculation, show your workings because some credit may be available for partially correct answers or for showing the correct method even if your answer is incorrect.

Now test yourself

TESTED ☐

5 Convert the following denary values to hexadecimal:
  (a) 26
  (b) 92
  (c) 175
6 Convert the following hexadecimal numbers to binary:
  (a) ABC
  (b) A5D
  (c) BBC3
7 Convert the following hexadecimal numbers to denary:
  (a) A5
  (b) 5F
  (c) 2DE

Answers on page 153

Images, sound and instructions

REVISED ☐

All data stored by the computer is in binary.

Images

Images are stored together with some **metadata** (data about the data). This metadata allows the computer to interpret the binary and reproduce the image.

Typically this will include information about the
- **colour depth**
- image **resolution**
- height and width in pixels.

The number of bits per pixel will determine how many colours can be represented:
- one bit: 2^1 or two colours
- two bits: 2^2 or four colours
- eight bits: 2^8 or 256 colours.

Metadata Information about the data that allows the computer to interpret the stored binary accurately to reproduce the original item.

Colour depth The number of bits used for each pixel.

Resolution The number of pixels used per unit, for example pixels per inch.

Example

Figure 11.1 **Coney Island**

More Info			
General	Exif	IPTC	JFIF	TIFF

Color Model **RGB**
Depth **8**
DPI Height **72**
DPI Width **72**
Orientation **1 (Normal)**
Pixel Height **1,536**
Pixel Width **2,048**
Profile Name **sRGB IEC61966-2.1**

Figure 11.2 **Basic data about the image of Coney Island**

Note in the data about the image the resolution is given in DPI (dots per inch); this is often seen for digital images rather than the more accurate PPI (pixels per inch).

Sound

Sound is sampled at various intervals and the data used to store an approximation to the sound.

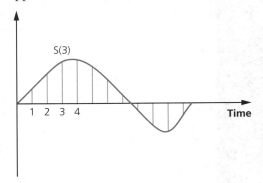

Figure 11.3 **An analogue signal is sampled at regular time intervals**

There are various factors that affect the quality of the sound stored.
- **Sample rate**: the number of times the sound is sampled per second measured in Hz.
- **Bit depth**: the number of bits used for each sample.
- **Bit rate**: the number of bits per given time period used to store the data.
- Bit rate = sample rate × bit depth.

Higher values means the stored sound will be of higher quality and more accurate but also means the file required to store them will be larger.

The size of a sound file can be calculated by

Size = Bit rate × number of channels × length of sample (in seconds)

Revision activity

Use a program such as Photoshop, IrfanView or GIMP to edit the resolution, size and colour depth of an image to see how each of these affects the size of the file needed to store the image.

Sample rate The number of times an analogue (continuously varying) signal is sampled (measured) per second, measured in hertz (Hz).

Bit depth The number of bits in each sample, which corresponds to the resolution of each sample.

Bit rate How much data is processed in a given amount of time, measured in kilobits per second.

Instructions

Program instructions and data are both stored by the computer in binary.

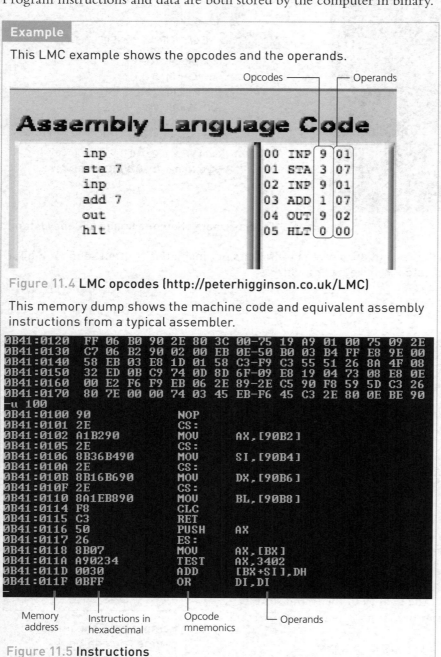

Example

This LMC example shows the opcodes and the operands.

Figure 11.4 **LMC opcodes (http://peterhigginson.co.uk/LMC)**

This memory dump shows the machine code and equivalent assembly instructions from a typical assembler.

Figure 11.5 **Instructions**

When a program is run:

1 The CPU is directed to the start address for the first instruction.
2 The binary number stored at that address is fetched and decoded into two parts: the operator (opcode) and the operand.
  ○ The **operator** is a binary pattern that represents a machine-level instruction, for example an instruction to add a value to the accumulator.
  ○ The **operand** is the data part and contains either a value to be dealt with or the information needed to locate the data to be dealt with, for example it might be the binary value for a location containing the data to be used.

> **Operator (opcode)** The part of a machine instruction that tells the computer what to do.
>
> **Operand** The part of a machine instruction that tells the computer what data to use with an operation.

3 The processor has no way of differentiating between data and instructions and interprets what it finds based on what it expects to find.
4 If it is told to run a program from a certain start location, it will interpret data it finds at that location as an instruction.
5 If there are errors in the program, it might fetch what is meant to be data but interpret it as an instruction.

Exam practice

1 Express the denary number 188 as:
   (a) a binary value   [2]
   (b) a hexadecimal value.   [2]
2 Why do programmers use hexadecimal?   [3]
3 Express the denary value –112 as an 8-bit binary value in:
   (a) sign and magnitude form   [2]
   (b) two's complement form.   [2]
4 What factors affect the file size for:
   (a) an image   [3]
   (b) a sound sample?   [3]
5 How does a computer distinguish between an instruction in a machine code program and data? [2]

Answers on page 164

Summary

- All data in a computer is stored in binary.
- The computer's character set is represented using Unicode; ASCII is a subset of Unicode that uses the same numeric representations.
- Boolean takes one of only two values, TRUE (1) or FALSE (0), often used as flags in programs.
- Integers are stored as either 'Sign and magnitude' form or, more commonly, in two's complement form. Two's complement is easier for the computer to process, using standard features in the processor.
- Hexadecimal is based on the number 16 and is used by programmers as a shorthand method to represent binary numbers. Hexadecimal converts easily from binary and is easier to remember, and mistakes with entering hexadecimal numbers are less likely than with binary.
- Images store metadata along with the image to allow the computer to interpret the image accurately, in terms of colour depth, resolution and dimensions. The larger these values, the more accurate the image, but this will increase the file size needed to store it.
- Sound is sampled at set intervals. The quality of the sound depends upon the sample rate and bit depth. The greater the accuracy, the larger the file.
- The processor cannot distinguish between data and instructions. It finds what it expects to find.

12 Computer arithmetic

Adding and subtracting integers in binary

REVISED

```
    00101101
+   10110111

    11100100

      11111   Carry
```
Check 45 + 183 = 228 ✓

```
       1 2
      02   2  Borrowing
    11100101
−   00001011

    11011010
```
Check 229 − 11 = 218 ✓

Exam tip

Do check the calculation in denary but it must be completed in binary showing the carrying and borrowing. There will be marks for showing your workings.

Now test yourself

TESTED

1 Complete the following additions and subtractions:
   (a) 10011 + 1011
   (b) 1110 + 1011
   (c) 11010 − 100
   (d) 10010 − 111
   (e) 10000 − 1011

Answers on page 153

Revision activity

There are a number of binary calculators on the internet, for example www.exploringbinary.com/binary-calculator/. You can create extra examples for addition, subtraction and conversion and check your answers using one of these calculators.

Adding using two's complement

Adding two's complement numbers is the same as adding standard non-signed integers but adding two large values illustrates the concept of **overflow**:

Overflow When the result of a calculation is too large to be represented accurately in the available space.

```
    01101100
+   01110000

    11011100
```
Check 108 + 112 = − 36 ✗

The two values when added together are too large to fit in the 8-bit two's complement format and overflow the space, giving a negative result.
● If the result of a calculation is too large to be stored it is called overflow.
● If the result of a calculation is too small to be stored it is called **underflow**.

Underflow When the result of a calculation is too small to be represented accurately in the available space.

Subtracting using two's complement

To subtract, we add the negative value of the number to be subtracted to the number we wish to subtract it from.

> **Example**
>
> For the denary example 79 − 51:
>
> | | |
> |---|---|
> | 51 in binary | 00110011 |
> | **one's complement** | 11001100 (change 1s to 0s and 0s to 1s) |
> | add one | 11001101 (this is two's complement for −51) |
> | 79 in binary | 01001111 |
> | add (1) | 00011100 (discard the overflow) |
>
> Check 79 − 51 = 28 ✓

One's complement Changing 1s to 0s and 0s to 1s in a binary value.

Now test yourself

TESTED

2 Use two's complement 8-bit binary to complete these calculations. Check your answers in denary.
   (a) 10110001 + 00011101
   (b) 10001111 + 01100011
3 Show these subtractions in two's complement binary form:
   (a) 67 − 35   (b) 108 − 66   (c) 53 − 65

Answers on page 153

Representing real numbers in binary

REVISED

Floating point is a similar concept to standard form as used in science and mathematics. In standard form, we represent numbers as a fraction raised to a power of 10, for example 1.236×10^2 to represent 123.6.

In floating point we use a binary fraction multiplied by a power of 2.

> **Example**
>
> The binary floating point number 0.101×2^{11}.
>
> This is the same as 0.101×2^3.
>
> Move the binary point three places to the right to get 101.0.
>
> This is 5 in denary.

For binary floating point we use two's complement **mantissa** with the most significant bit set to −1, the rest to fractional values, $\frac{1}{2}$, $\frac{1}{4}$, and so on.

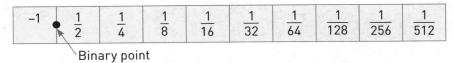

Binary point

Mantissa The part of the floating point number that represents the significant digits of that number.

Exponent The power to which the number in the mantissa is to be raised.

The **exponent** is a two's complement integer.

−32	16	8	4	2	1

Example

The binary floating point number 0110100000 000010

is the same as 0.110100000×2^2.

Move the binary point two places to the right to get:

11.01 or 3.25 in denary.

Example

The binary floating point number 0110000000 111111

is the same as 0.11×2^{-1}.

Move the binary point one place to the left to get:

0.011 or 0.375 in denary.

If the first bit of the mantissa is 1 then it is a negative number.

Example

1010100000 000011

We convert the mantissa to a sign and magnitude form by:

1's complement	0101011111
add 1	0101100000

(This is the unsigned magnitude of the mantissa.)

Now adjust for the exponent, 11 in binary, by moving the binary point three places to the right.

We get the value 0101.100000.

This is the magnitude of the negative value 5.5, so

1010100000 000011 is equal to −5.5 in denary.

> **Exam tip**
>
> These examples use 10-bit mantissa and 6-bit exponent, both in two's complement, but check carefully the format used by the examiner for the question, it may not be the same.

Now test yourself

TESTED ☐

4 Using an 8-bit floating point number with 5-bit mantissa and 3-bit exponent in two's complement form, convert the following to denary:
   (a) 01010 001
   (b) 10110 010
   (c) 01100 111
5 Using a 16-bit floating point number with 10-bit mantissa and 6-bit exponent in two's complement form, convert the following to denary:
   (a) 0101100000 000011
   (b) 1011000000 111111

Answers on page 153

Normalisation of floating point numbers

With floating point numbers there is a balance between accuracy and range.
- More bits for the mantissa improves the accuracy of the representation but reduces the range of values that can be represented.
- More bits for the exponent improves the range of values but reduces the accuracy of the value represented.

In order to improve the accuracy, the mantissa should not waste bits by having redundant digits at the start of a value.
- For a positive mantissa, after the leading 0, the mantissa is floated so that this 0 is followed by a 1.
- For a negative mantissa, after the leading 1, the mantissa is floated so that this 1 is followed by a 0.
- This is done by adjusting the exponent.
- Once the binary point is floated to the right place:
  - positive mantissas are padded with 0s
  - negative mantissas are padded with 1s.

Example

Using an 8-bit floating point with five bits for the mantissa and three for the exponent.

In the binary fraction 0.0011 we need to float the binary point two places to the right so need an exponent of −2.

(In 3-bit two's complement −2 is represented by 110.)

0.0011 is written as 0.1100 110 in normalised floating point form.

- A normalised floating point number will always start with either 01 or 10.

Now test yourself

6 Using a 16-bit floating point number with 10-bit mantissa and 6-bit exponent in two's complement form, represent the following denary values in normalised floating point form:
   (a) 1.625
   (b) −2.5
   (c) 0.1875

Answers on page 153

Adding and subtracting floating point numbers

To add and subtract floating point numbers, we use the exponent to align the binary points then add or subtract in the same way as standard two's complement numbers.

Example

Using a 5-bit mantissa and 3-bit exponent.

01011 001 + 01100 010

In 01011 001 the exponent is 1 so we move the binary point one place to the right: 01.011.

In 01100 010 the exponent is 2 so we move the binary point two places to the right: 011.00:

We align the binary points and padding 0s then add:

```
     01.011
  +  11.00
    100.011
```

01010 010 – 01100 001

Undoing the exponents, the calculation becomes:

```
    010.10
  -  01.100
     01.000
```

Now test yourself

7 Using 8-bit floating point with a 5-bit mantissa and 3-bit exponent in two's complement form, complete the following calculations:
   (a) 01110 001 + 01010 011
   (b) 01010 111 + 01100 001
   (c) 01101 010 – 01011 001
   (d) 01010 111 – 01100 110

Answers on page 153

Bitwise manipulation of binary values

Shifting

A logical shift left or right moves each bit of the binary value left or right (filling any vacated spaces with 0).

Example

For the binary value:

0	0	1	1	0	1	0	0

A logical shift left by two moves the whole number to the left two places:

1	1	0	1	0	0	0	0

A logical shift right by one moves the whole number to the right one place:

0	0	0	1	1	0	1	0

Calculating the values of the binary integers above:

00110100 in denary   52

11010000 in denary   208 (52×2^2)

00011010 in denary   26 $(52 \div 2^1)$

- A shift left multiplies by 2 for each place.
- A shift right divides by 2 for each place.

Logical operations and masking

The ALU can perform bitwise operations using the standard logical operators, NOT, AND, OR and XOR.

Example

NOT is applied to each bit in the binary to reverse the value of that bit.

0	0	1	1	0	1	0	0

NOT

1	1	0	0	1	0	1	1

Example

For AND, OR and XOR the operation is applied to matching bits in two binary numbers, the operand and the mask, to determine each bit in the resultant binary value.

Operand	0	0	1	1	0	1	0	0
Mask	1	1	1	1	0	0	0	0
AND	0	0	1	1	0	0	0	0

Operand	0	0	1	1	0	1	0	0
Mask	1	1	1	1	0	0	0	0
OR	1	1	1	1	0	1	0	0

Operand	0	0	1	1	0	1	0	0
Mask	1	1	1	1	0	0	0	0
XOR	1	1	0	0	0	1	0	0

Masking is a very important concept that allows the CPU to manipulate individual bits in the operand, checking for values, allowing bits through or blocking them.

- AND is useful for checking conditions stored in a binary value.
  - Masking with a 1 returns the operand bit value.
  - Masking with a 0 excludes the operand bit.
- OR can reset individual bits in a binary value.
  - Masking with 1 will always set the returned bit to 1.
  - Masking with 0 returns the original operand bit value.
- XOR will check that two bits are not the same (that is, return 1 if the bits are different, 0 if they're the same).
  - If both mask and operand are the same it returns 0.
  - If mask and operand are different it returns 1.

Now test yourself

TESTED ☐

8 Using the operand 00110110, mask this with 10101010 using AND, OR and XOR.

9 Create a mask to reverse the first, fourth and last digits of an operand. State which logical operand is required.

10 Create a mask to check if the second, fifth and last bits of an operand are set to 1. State which logical operation is required.

Answers on page 153

Exam practice

1 Subtract the binary integer 11011 from 100000. [2]
2 Show the two's complement binary process for the subtraction 72 – 47. [5]
3 Convert the 8-bit floating point number 11000 111 (5-bit mantissa and 3-bit exponent) to denary. [2]
4 Using a normalised 8-bit floating point number with 5-bit mantissa and 3-bit exponent, calculate:
   (a) 01110 010 + 01100 001 [2]
   (b) 01010 001 + 01100 000 [2]
   (c) 01110 001 – 01100 111 [2]
5 Mask the operand 10110110 with 1111000 and the logical operation OR. What effect does this have on the operand? [2]

Answers on page 164

Summary

- Adding and subtracting integers in binary is similar to denary, but the place values are 2, 4, 8 ...; 1+1=10 and 1+1+1=11 in base 2.
- Overflow is when the result of a calculation is too large to fit in the allocated space.
- Underflow is when the result of a calculation is too small to fit in the allocated space.
- Real numbers are represented in floating point form using a mantissa and exponent. The mantissa represents the significant digits; the exponent represents the power of 2 the mantissa is raised to.
- Floating point numbers are normalised to ensure the maximum number of significant digits can be stored.

- To add and subtract floating point numbers, first undo the exponent and line up the binary points.
- Shifting a binary integer left multiplies it by 2 for each place.
- Shifting a binary integer right divides it by 2 for each place.
- Binary data can be masked using logical operators: NOT, AND, OR and XOR:
  - NOT reverses the digits.
  - AND is useful for checking conditions stored in a binary value.
  - OR can reset individual bits in a binary value.
  - XOR can be used to check if corresponding bits in the operand and mask are the same.

13 Data structures

Records, lists and tuples

Each of these structures contains data to be processed: records, lists and tuples.

Record

- A record is accessed through an attribute.
- A record is an unordered data structure.
- Indices may be programmed to provide the data ordered on a particular attribute.
- The ability to access data through an attribute makes the record structure more user friendly.
- The need to define all the attributes before use makes the record structure more complex to initialise.

> **Example**
>
> In an address book the attributes may be:
>
> `first _ name, last _ name, address1, address2, post _ code, telephone, email,` and so on.
>
> The data is accessible through each of these attributes.
>
> For example `address _ book.last _ name`.

List

- A list is an ordered data structure.
- A list is accessed through an index.
- The index indicates the position of the data in the list.
- Lists have no pre-defined scope (number of elements).
- Not needing to define attributes in advance makes the list easier to initialise than a record.
- Accessing the data in order by index is straightforward to program.

> **Example**
>
> In an address book organised as a list, data is found by its position in the list.
>
> `address _ book(5)` would return the data at position 5 in the list.

Tuple

- A tuple is a list.
- A tuple is immutable; that is, the data cannot be modified.
- Tuples are useful for data that must be accessed by index but must not be changed.

Arrays

Arrays are data structures that store data using indices.

One-dimensional arrays

- One-dimensional arrays are similar to a list but have a defined scope (number of elements).
- A one-dimensional array defines a set of variables under a single descriptor with an index.

> **Arrays** Structures that store data under a single identifier by index.

Example

An array defined under the descriptor names with scope 5 will create five variables:

names(0), names(1), names(2), names(3) and names(4)

This array may contain the data:

names(0)	names(1)	names(2)	names(3)	names(4)
Frank	Hameed	Yin	Hannah	Marta

Accessing names(2) will return Yin.

Changing names(1) to Umar will modify the array to:

names(0)	names(1)	names(2)	names(3)	names(4)
Frank	Umar	Yin	Hannah	Marta

Multi-dimensional arrays

- A two-dimensional array creates a structure that allows access to the data by two indices similar to (x,y) co-ordinates in a table, where *x* refers to the row and *y* the column in a two-dimensional table.

Example

Names()	0	1	2	3	4
0	Billy	Johan	Navdeep	Graham	Hua
1	Frank	Hameed	Yin	Hannah	Marta
2	Barry	Wayne	Tracey	Kylie	David
3	Irina	Li	Sundip	Tomasz	Dillip
4	Deborah	James	Michael	Wendy	Charles

Accessing names(2,3) returns Kylie.

- A three-dimensional array, for example, will allow access to data through three indices similar to co-ordinates in three dimensions (x,y,z).

Stacks and queues

Stacks and **queues** are implementations of lists that store data in a linear ordered fashion. These structures have specific methods for inserting and removing data.

> **Stack** Last In First Out data structure.
>
> **Queue** First In First Out data structure.

Stacks

- Data is added to the top of the structure.
- Data is removed from the top of the structure.
- Stacks are Last In First Out (LIFO) data structures.
- PUSH is the command to insert data.
- POP is the command to remove data.

Example

A stack initially contains:

23   ←Top

13

4   ←Bottom

PUSH 7 results in 7 being added to the top of the stack:

7   ←Top

23

13

4   ←Bottom

PUSH 18 results in 18 being added to the top of the stack:

18   ←Top

7

23

13

4   ←Bottom

POP results in the data at the top of the stack being removed, leaving:

7   ←Top

23

13

4   ←Bottom

- We call the top pointer the 'stack pointer'.

Algorithms

If a stack is full, data cannot be pushed to it.

An algorithm to describe a PUSH operation is:

```
If stack pointer maximum then report stack full.
Else
    Set the stack pointer to stack pointer +1
    Set stack(stack pointer) to data
Endif
```

If a stack becomes empty, data cannot be popped from it.

An algorithm to describe a POP operation is:

```
If stack pointer bottom then report stack empty
Else
    Set data to stack(stack pointer)
    Set stack pointer to stack pointer -1
Endif
```

Exam tip

It is worth learning the algorithms but they need not be repeated in the form shown. Try to make sense of what is happening in these algorithms, write them in plain English and remember that.

Queues

- Data is added to the end of the structure.
- Data is removed from the start of the structure.
- Queues are First In First Out (FIFO) data structures.
- PUSH is the command to insert data.
- POP is the command to remove data.

Example

A queue initially contains:

23 ←Start

13

4 ←End

PUSH 7 results in 7 being added to the end of the queue.

23 ←Start

13

4

7 ←End

PUSH 18 results in 18 being added to the end of the queue.

23 ←Start

13

4

7

18 ←End

POP results in the data at the start of the queue being removed leaving.

13 ←Start

4

7

18 ←End

Queues are often circular so that data added at the end of the queue can be stored in locations vacated at the start of the queue.

Example

Initially a queue has this data:

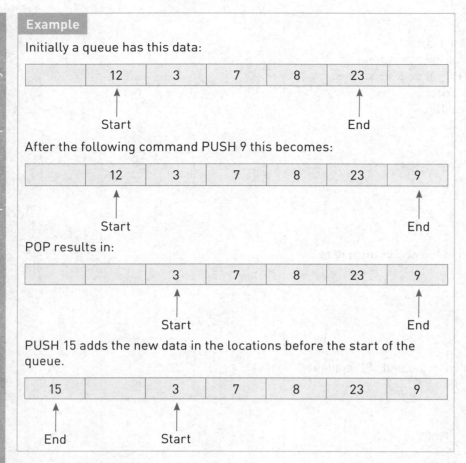

After the following command PUSH 9 this becomes:

POP results in:

PUSH 15 adds the new data in the locations before the start of the queue.

Algorithms

If a queue is full, data cannot be pushed to it.

An algorithm to describe a **PUSH** operation is:

```
If the start pointer = 1 and the end pointer =
maximum then report that the queue is full
Elseif the start pointer = the endpointer+1 report
that the queue is full
Else
     Add data at end pointer+1
     Set end pointer to end pointer+1
Endif
```

If a queue is empty, data cannot be popped from it.

An algorithm to describe a **POP** operation is:

```
If start pointer = 0 then report queue empty
Else
     data = queue(start pointer)
     set start pointer to start pointer+1
Endif
```

Consider:
- If the start pointer = the end pointer there is only 1 item in the queue.
- If this item is removed, the start pointer should be reset to 0.
- If the start pointer points to the maximum value for the queue then it needs to be reset to point at the data item at the start of the structure.

PUSH Command to add data to a queue or stack.

POP Command to remove data from a queue or stack.

Revision activity

There are various animations for data structures available on the internet. Being able to add and remove data from these animations will improve the appreciation of the process. Daniel Liang from Armstrong University has a website with interactive animations for several data structures: http://cs.armstrong.edu/liang/animation/animation.html

When these situations are accounted for the algorithm becomes:

```
If start pointer = 0 then report queue empty
Else
     data = queue(start pointer)
     If start pointer = end pointer then
        start pointer = 0
        end pointer = 0
     Endif
     If start pointer = maximum then
        start pointer = 1
     Else start pointer = start pointer+1
     Endif
Endif
```

Now test yourself

TESTED ☐

1 A stack contains 3, 7, 12, with the 3 being the first value stored and 12 the last. Show how the stack changes when the following sequence of commands is used:
PUSH 9
POP
POP
PUSH 17
POP
POP

2 A queue contains 5, 3, 7, where 5 is at the start of the queue and 7 at the end. Show how the queue changes when the following sequence of commands is used:
PUSH 12
POP
POP
PUSH 9
POP
PUSH 6

3 In the array names(), where names(r, c) refers to the data at row r and column c:

Names()	0	1	2	3	4	5
0	Alan	Kuldeep	Li	Sarah	Harry	Mary
1	Jane	Tomasz	Charles	Thomas	Jane	Irina
2	Wendy	Deborah	Dillip	Umar	Johan	Hua

(a) What is stored in the variable names(1, 4)?
(b) Show what happens to the array when:
   (i) names(1, 3) is set to Joe
   (ii) names(1, 1) is set to Navdeep.
(c) After these changes have been made, what is output by the following program?

```
For x=1 to 3
     Output names(1,x)
Next x
```

Answers on page 154

Linked lists

REVISED

A **linked list** is a list of data together with a set of links to sort the data on various factors. Data is stored in the order it is input and pointers are used to link the data in the desired order.

> **Linked list** Unordered data structure that uses pointers to sort the data.

Example

Data item	Fruit
1	Strawberry
2	Banana
3	Apple
4	Damson
5	Cherry

- By adding pointers, these items can be sorted alphabetically.
- We need a start pointer to point to the first item.
- We need a pointer from each item to point to the next one in the sorted list.
- We need an end pointer to show that we have reached the last item in the sorted list.
- We use the data item 0 as an end pointer.

Data item	Fruit	Start (3) Alpha pointers
1	Strawberry	0
2	Banana	5
3	Apple	2
4	Damson	1
5	Cherry	4

This can be shown in a diagram.

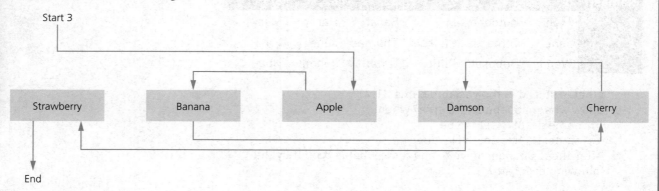

Figure 13.1

The data may also be sorted on other factors, for example the weight of the individual item. To do this we simply add another set of pointers.

Data item	Fruit	Start (3) Alpha pointers	Start (5) Weight pointers
1	Strawberry	0	4
2	Banana	5	0
3	Apple	2	2
4	Damson	1	3
5	Cherry	4	1

Adding data to a linked list

Additional data is inserted at the next available free node. There is a pointer called 'free storage pointer' that points to the first available free location.

Example

For this linked list:

Data item	Fruit	Start (3) Free (6) Alpha pointers
1	Strawberry	0
2	Banana	5
3	Apple	2
4	Damson	1
5	Cherry	4
6		
7		
8		
9		

To add orange to the list:
- Orange is added to the location indicated by the free storage pointer (6).
- The free storage pointer is updated to the next free location (7).
- The location in the list is identified (it follows Damson).
- The pointer for this location is updated to point to the location for the new data item (6).
- The pointer for the new item is updated to that previously stored in the item that preceded it (1).

The list becomes:

Data item	Fruit	Start (3) Free (7) Alpha pointers
1	Strawberry	0
2	Banana	5
3	Apple	2
4	Damson	**6**
5	Cherry	4
6	Orange	**1**
7		
8		
9		

Removing data from a linked list

To remove data from a linked list the pointers to that data are removed and the data bypassed.

Example

Removing 'Cherry' from this data:

Data item	Fruit	Start (3) Free (7) Alpha pointers
1	Strawberry	0
2	Banana	5
3	Apple	2
4	Damson	**6**
5	Cherry	4
6	Orange	**1**
7		
8		
9		

- The pointer for the item preceding Cherry is updated to the pointer at the node Cherry (pointer at node 2, Banana, becomes 4).
- The node for the deleted item is added to the free storage location list.

Data item	Fruit	Start (3) Free (7) Alpha pointers
1	Strawberry	0
2	Banana	**4**
3	Apple	2
4	Damson	6
5	Cherry	
6	Orange	1
7		
8		
9		

Free pointers	7	8	9	**5**

Exam tip

You may be asked to draw these diagrams. It is a good idea to start with the table of pointers then draw the diagram based on that information. It is much easier to keep track of the data in the table.

Showing the results of all of these changes on a diagram:

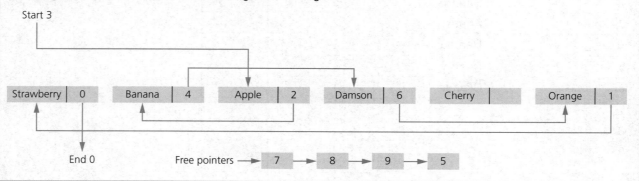

13 Data structures

Algorithms

Traversing a linked list to output the date items in order:

```
Set the pointer to the start value
Repeat
     Go to node(pointer value)
     Output data at node
     Set the pointer to value of next item pointer
at the node
Until pointer = 0
```

It is also useful to be able to locate an item in a linked list:

```
Set the pointer to the start value
Repeat
     Go to node(pointer value)
     IF data at node is search item
        output and stop
     Else
        Set the pointer to value of next item pointer
        at the node
     Endif
Until pointer = 0
Output data item not found
```

Now test yourself

TESTED

4 The data Monkey, Lion, Cheetah, Zebra, Gorilla is stored as a linked list in that order.

The list is sorted alphabetically.
(a) Show the data in the original order and the pointers used to sort the list.
(b) Show this data with Lion removed.
(c) Show this list with Tiger added.

Answers on page 154

Trees

REVISED

For data that does not fit into a list, for example the directory structure on a computer hard drive, we need hierarchical data structures such as **trees**.

> **Tree** Hierarchical data structure with data related to the data above it in the tree.

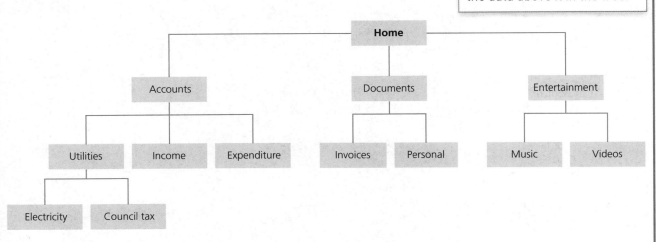

Figure 13.2 **A tree structure**

- The node at the start of the structure is called the root node.
- The nodes immediately down from another node are called children.
- The nodes with children are called parents.
- The lines that join the notes are called branches.

Binary trees

One specific kind of tree is the **binary tree**, where each node is only allowed to have two children. Each node contains:

- a left pointer
- data
- a right pointer.

> **Binary tree** Tree structure where each node can only have two branches: left and right.

Example

Using the data Cherry, Apple, Damson, Banana we can create a binary tree to store the data alphabetically.
- Left pointer to data that precedes the data in the current node.
- Right pointer to data that comes after the data in the current node.

Putting Cherry as the root node, Apple precedes it so goes to the left.

The next item is Damson, which comes after Cherry so it goes to the right.

Banana precedes Cherry so we go left.

Banana comes after Apple so we go to the right of Apple.

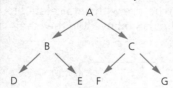

Example

There are various ways to retrieve the data from a binary tree.

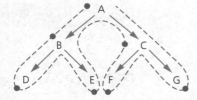

Preorder

1 Start at root node.
2 Traverse the left sub-tree.
3 Traverse the right sub-tree.

This gives the output for the tree above: ABDECFG.

Inorder

1 Traverse the left sub-tree.
2 Visit the root node.
3 Traverse the right sub-tree.

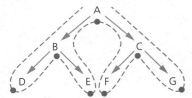

This gives the output for the tree above: DBEAFCG.

Postorder

1 Traverse the left sub-tree.
2 Traverse the right sub-tree.
3 Return to the root node.

This gives the output for the tree above: DEBFGCA.

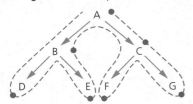

Exam tip

The binary trees described all use left for preceding and right for following. These are called left-hand trees. Be careful to read the question and make sure they are not specifically asking for a right-hand tree.

Now test yourself

TESTED

5 The data Monkey, Lion, Cheetah, Zebra, Gorilla, Tiger is stored in a binary tree, with the left branch preceding the node alphabetically and right branch following alphabetically.
  (a) Put this data into a tree structure.
  (b) Show the data retrieved using preorder traversal.
  (c) Show the data retrieved using postorder traversal.

Answers on page 154

Graphs

REVISED

A **graph** is a collection of data nodes with connections between them.
- The data nodes are called vertices.
- The connections are called edges.
- Edges may be assigned weightings.
- A graph may be directional or undirected.
- In a directed graph the data connection may flow in one or both directions.
- In an undirected graph the edges are all bi-directional.

Graph Mathematical data structure consisting of vertices and edges joining these vertices. Graphs are used in computer science to model real-world systems such as the internet, airline connections and road networks.

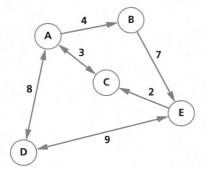

Figure 13.3 A directional graph

A graph can be described as a set of ordered pairs showing the edges and the weightings:

{(A,B,4),(A,C,3),(A,D,8),(B,E,7),(C,A,3),(D,A,8),(D,E,9),(E,C,2),(E,D,9)}

A graph can also be described by an adjacency matrix:

	A	B	C	D	E
A		4	3	8	
B					7
C	3				
D	8				9
E			2	9	

Traversing graphs

Depth-first

- Depth-first traversal uses a stack to store the visited nodes.
- Visit all nodes attached to a node connected to a starting node before visiting a second node attached to a starting node.

Algorithm

```
PUSH the first node onto the stack
Mark as visited
Repeat
    Visit the next unvisited node to the one on top
    of the stack
    Mark as visited
    PUSH this node onto the stack
    If no node to visit POP node off the stack
Until the stack is empty
```

Example

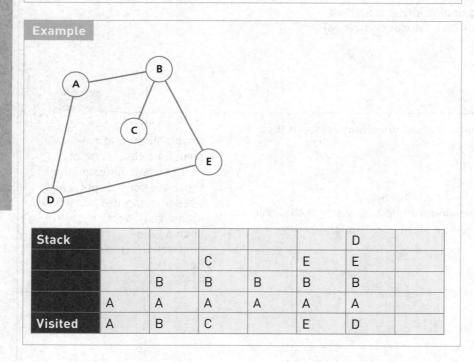

Stack					D	
		C		E	E	
	B	B	B	B	B	
	A	A	A	A	A	
Visited	A	B	C		E	D

13 Data structures

Breadth-first

- Breadth-first traversal uses a queue to store the visited nodes.
- Visit all the nodes attached directly to a starting node first.

Algorithm

```
PUSH the first node into the queue
Mark as visited
Repeat
     Visit unvisited nodes connected to first node
     PUSH nodes onto queue
Until all nodes visited
Repeat
     POP next node from queue
     Repeat
        Visit unvisited nodes connected to current
        node
        PUSH nodes onto queue
     Until all nodes visited
Until queue empty
```

Example

Queue		B	B	D	D	D	C	E	
			D		C	C	E		
						E			
Visited	A	B	D		C	E			
Current	A	A	A	B	B	B	D	C	E

Now test yourself

TESTED ☐

6 Draw the graph represented by this adjacency matrix.

	A	B	C	D	E	F
A		6	5			
B	6					
C				7		
D			7		4	
E						2
F		3			2	

7 For the undirected graph shown below, show the results of:
   (a) depth-first traversal
   (b) breadth-first traversal.

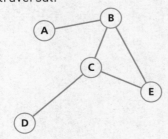

Answers on page 154

Hash tables

Hash tables are used to access data that is stored in a more random manner. Each item maps to an address in a table containing data about that item. One example is mail order accounts that are accessed randomly as customers contact the company. Data can be accessed through their customer account number.

- Simple **hash functions** such as account _ number mod 1000 will generate clashes.
- Duplicated values would be stored at the same address in an overflow table as either an unordered table or as a linked list with the address as the start pointer.

> **Hash function** Applied to a field to calculate a storage address for the data associated with that item.

Typically hash functions are much more complex, but some simple examples are:

address =(k*k) mod m or address = k(k+3) mod m

where k is the key value and m is the number of locations or 'buckets'. If m is chosen carefully it can improve the efficiency of the algorithms. For example, m could be a prime number close to a power of 2.

Example

For 100 accounts:

The closest power of 2 is 128.

The closest prime to 128 is 127.

We can choose m to be 127.

For account number 100:

100*100 mod 127

= 10000 mod 127

= 94

We use address 94 for account 100.

Now test yourself

8 Using the **hashing** function k(k+3) mod m
where k is the key field and m is the bucket size,
if m is 251, calculate the addresses for the key fields:
(a) 101
(b) 52

> **Hashing** A method for creating random access to stored data.

Answers on page 154

Exam practice

1 The items 5, 7, 2, 8, 4 are stored in a linked list.
  (a) Draw the table showing these items sorted numerically using pointers. [3]
  (b) Draw the diagram showing the data stored in a linked list sorted numerically [3]
  (c) Modify the diagram to show the item 8 removed from this linked list. [2]
2 The items 8, 12, 19, 6, 14, 5, 7 are stored in a binary tree.
  Draw the left-hand tree for this data. [3]
3 Draw the graph represented by the order pairs:

  {(A,B,5),(B,A,5),(B,D,4),(C,B,3),(C.E,2),(D,B,4),(D.E,6),(E,D,6)} [3]
4 Show the traversal of the following graph using depth-first and breadth-first traversal methods. [8]

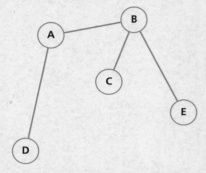

5 Where k is the key value and m is 113, find the locations used to store the data with key field 57 using the hashing algorithm k*k mod m. [2]

Answers on page 165

Summary

- A record is an unordered data structure accessed by an attribute. The attributes must be defined before the structure is used. Using attributes makes the structure more user-friendly.
- Lists are ordered data structures accessed by using an index that represents the position of data in the list. Lists have no pre-defined scope (size) and are easier to define since there is no need for attributes. Because they use an index to access data, lists are straightforward to program.
- Arrays define a set of variables under a single descriptor with an index. Two-dimensional arrays have two indices similar to co-ordinates (row and column). Three-dimensional arrays use three indices.
- Stacks are Last In First Out (LIFO) data structures. Data is added to and removed from the top of the stack.
- Queues are First In First Out (FIFO) data structures. Data is added to the front of, and removed from, the end of a queue. Queues are often circular so that data added at the end of the queue can be stored in locations vacated at the start of the queue.
- Linked lists use pointers to sort data by pointing at the next item in the list. They use a start pointer and an end pointer that usually points to 0 or null. Linked lists can have multiple sets of pointers to sort data on various attributes.

- Trees are hierarchical structures used to store data that does not fit into a list. The start node is called the 'root node', nodes immediately down from another node are called 'children', nodes with children are called 'parents' and the links between nodes are called 'branches'.
- A binary tree allows only two branches from each node: a left and a right pointer.
- Binary trees can be traversed in three ways: inorder, preorder and postorder
- Graphs are a mathematical data structure consisting of data nodes (vertices) and links between nodes (edges). Graphs can be undirected or directed. Directed graphs can be uni-directional or bi-directional.
- Graphs can be traversed in two ways: depth-first using a stack to visit all nodes attached to a starting node before visiting a second node, or breadth-first using a queue to visit all nodes directly connected to a starting node first.
- Hash algorithms are used to locate data stored in a random manner. An attribute of the data is processed using a suitable algorithm to identify a suitable location. If calculated locations clash, then data is stored in a linked list starting at that location or simply as a list stored at that location.

14 Logic gates and Boolean algebra

Logic gates

REVISED

AND ∧		
A	B	R
0	0	0
0	1	0
1	0	0
1	1	1

Figure 14.1 Truth table and symbol for AND gate

OR ∨		
A	B	R
0	0	0
0	1	1
1	0	1
1	1	1

Figure 14.2 Truth table and symbol for OR gate

NOT¬	
A	R
0	1
1	0

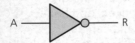

Figure 14.3 Truth table and symbol for NOT gate

Logic gates can be combined into more complex functions and we can use a truth table to calculate the output from these functions.

Example

R = ¬(A ∨ B) ∧ C

Truth table showing all possibilities:

R = ¬(A ∨ B) ∧ C					
A	B	C	A∨B	¬(A∨B)	R
0	0	0	0	1	0
0	0	1	0	1	1
0	1	0	1	0	0
0	1	1	1	0	0
1	0	0	1	0	0
1	0	1	1	0	0
1	1	0	1	0	0
1	1	1	1	0	0

By looking at the truth table we can see that:

¬(A ∨ B) ∧ C is the same as ¬ A ∧ ¬ B ∧ C.

Now test yourself

TESTED

1 Complete the truth tables for these expressions:
   (a) (A ∧ B) ∨ ¬ C
   (b) ¬ (A ∧ B) ∨ C
2 Draw the logic circuits for these expressions also.

Answers on page 155

Boolean operations are carried out in order of precedence NOT, AND then OR.

There are rules to manipulate Boolean expressions and 0 (nothing) and 1 (everything) are defined:

● ¬ (¬A) = A   (double negative law)
● A ∧ ¬A = 0   (complement law)
● A ∨ ¬A = 1   (complement law)

There are three more important logic gates:

NAND		
A	B	R
0	0	1
0	1	1
1	0	1
1	1	0

Figure 14.4 Truth table and symbol for NAND gate

Revision activity

There is another way to solve Boolean algebra problems using Venn diagrams:

Circles represent the values A, B and C. Where A and B overlap is A ∧ B, the whole area contained by both A and B is A ∨ B, and so on. This gives a visual representation of the Boolean expression. To find out more about this, search on the internet for 'Boolean algebra and Venn diagrams'. One example site is: www.allaboutcircuits.com/textbook/digital/chpt-8/boolean-relationships-on-venn-diagrams/

NOR		
A	B	R
0	0	1
0	1	0
1	0	0
1	1	0

Figure 14.5 Truth table and symbol for NOR gate

XOR		
A	B	R
0	0	0
0	1	1
1	0	1
1	1	0

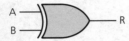

Figure 14.6 Truth table and symbol for XOR gate

Karnaugh maps

REVISED

Karnaugh maps:
- use pattern recognition to simplify Boolean expressions
- are tables of possible inputs mapped against outputs
- use a slightly different order for inputs to make pattern recognition more effective.

Example

Three-input Karnaugh map:

c\AB	00	01	11	10
0	1	1	0	0
1	1	1	1	1

The blue block is ¬A.

The red block is C.

The expression is therefore ¬A ∨ C.

Four-input Karnaugh map:

CD\AB	00	01	11	10
00	1	0	1	1
01	1	0	0	0
11	1	0	0	0
10	1	0	1	1

The blue block is ¬A ∧ ¬B.

The red block wraps around and is A ∧ ¬D.

Therefore the expression is (¬A ∧ ¬B) ∨ (A ∧ ¬D).

The rules for Karnaugh maps are:
- no zeros allowed in the blocks
- no diagonal blocks
- groups as large as possible
- groups must contain 1, 2, 4, 8, and so on, 1s in a block
- overlapping blocks are allowed
- wrap around blocks are allowed
- aim for the smallest possible number of groups.

Now test yourself

TESTED ☐

3 Simplify the expression shown in these Karnaugh maps:

(a)

CD\AB	00	01	11	10
00	1	1	1	1
01	1	1	0	0
11	0	0	0	0
10	0	0	0	0

(b)

CD\AB	00	01	11	10
00	0	0	0	0
01	0	1	1	0
11	1	1	1	1
10	1	0	0	1

4 By completing a Karnaugh map, simplify the expression:
$(\neg A \wedge B) \vee (B \wedge \neg C) \vee (B \wedge C) \vee (A \wedge \neg B \wedge \neg C)$

Answers on page 155

> ### Revision activity
>
> There are a number of Boolean algebra calculators on the internet. Try this search string in your chosen search engine: Wolfram alpha Boolean algebra calculator widget. This widget shows the truth table, the minimal form, a logic circuit and a Venn diagram. You can create more examples for yourself and check your answers.

A Level only

Boolean algebra operations

REVISED ☐

There are a number of rules similar to those for standard arithmetic operators + and × .

Associative $\quad (A \wedge B) \wedge C = A \wedge (B \wedge C)$

$\qquad\qquad (A \vee B) \vee C = A \vee (B \vee C)$

Commutative $\quad A \wedge B = B \wedge A$

$\qquad\qquad A \vee B = B \vee A$

Distributive $\quad A \wedge (B \vee C) = (A \wedge B) \vee (A \wedge C)$

There are also some simplification rules for Boolean algebra.

De Morgan's rules

$\neg(A \vee B) = \neg A \wedge \neg B$

$\neg(A \wedge B) = \neg A \vee \neg B$

These rules can be used to simplify expressions.

Example

C ∨ ¬(B∧C)	Original expression
C ∨ ¬B ∨ ¬C	De Morgan
(C ∨ ¬C) ∨ ¬B	Commutative and associative laws
1 ∨ ¬B	Complement law
1	Identity

Exam tip

If the exam question asks you to use a particular method then do so, otherwise use whichever method you are most comfortable with. You can always check answers using your preferred method if time allows.

Now test yourself

TESTED

5 Simplify the expressions:
   (a) (A ∧ B) ∨ (A ∧ C)
   (b) (A ∧ B) ∨ A ∧ (B ∨ C)
   (c) ¬A ∨ C ∨ (A ∧ B)

Answers on page 155

Adder circuits

REVISED

A half-adder is a logic circuit with two inputs and two outputs: the sum and carry when the two inputs are added in binary. The truth table is:

A	B	S	C
0	0	0	0
0	1	1	0
1	0	1	0
1	1	0	1

From this table it is clear:
- S is A XOR B
- C is A AND B.

This circuit is a half adder:

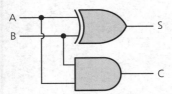

Figure 14.7 A half-adder

A full adder allows the carry from a previous calculation to be carried forward in the calculation. To deal with carries from previous calculations there would need to be three inputs, A, B and C_{in}. It would need to produce two outputs S and C_{out}. The truth table is:

A	B	C_{in}	S	C_{out}
0	0	0	0	0
0	0	1	1	0
0	1	0	1	0
0	1	1	0	1
1	0	0	1	0
1	0	1	0	1
1	1	0	0	1
1	1	1	1	1

Exam tip

Learn the diagrams for half-adder, adder and D-Type flip-flop and remember the key points.

Using two half adders and an OR gate to combine C1 and C2, we get a full adder.

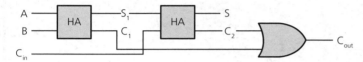

Figure 14.8 A full adder

A series of full adders connected together allows the computer to add binary numbers.

Flip-flop circuits

REVISED

There are some important circuits that differ from the gate circuits we have considered so far. These circuits are capable of storing information, for example RAM memory.

Consider this basic circuit:

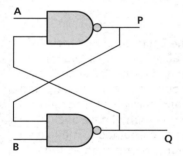

Figure 14.9 A basic circuit

The truth table for this differs from the others we have seen because when A is 1 and B is 1 there are two possibilities:

A	B	P	Q
0	0	1	1
0	1	1	0
1	0	0	1
1	1	0	1
		1	0

This circuit can exist in either state; which state depends upon the previous values stored. This circuit is called a flip-flop and it can store one bit of information. By combining flip-flops we can create a number of circuits.

Two flip-flops combined to make a D-type flip-flop.

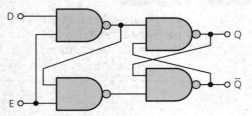

Figure 14.10 D-type flip-flop

The D stands for delay and the D-type flip-flop:
- uses a clock pulse to delay the output
- has two inputs
  - data
  - clock
- has two outputs, the
  - data
  - inverse of the data.

Exam practice

1 Simplify the expressions:
   (a) ¬(A ∨ B) ∧ (A ∨ C)   [3]
   (b) (A ∧ B) ∨ (B ∧ C) ∧ (B ∨ C)   [2]
   (c) (A ∨ C) ∧ (B ∨ C)   [1]

Answers on page 166

Summary

- There are six logic gates – NOT, AND, OR, XOR, NAND and NOR– for which you should know the truth table and logic circuit symbol.
- A Boolean expression consists of inputs, A, B, C, and so on, combined using these logic gates. The symbols used to represent the logic gates are ¬ (NOT), ∧ (AND) and ∨ (OR).
- Karnaugh maps use pattern recognition to simplify Boolean expression. They are tables of all possible inputs mapped against the required outputs. By identifying blocks of 1s and the equivalent Boolean expression, the original expression may be simplified. Blocks must only be blocks of two, four, eight, and so on 1s; there should be no 0s in the blocks.
- There are standard rules for Boolean algebra similar to those for mathematical algebra that can be applied to simplifying expressions. These include double negative; complement; associative; commutative and distributive laws; and De Morgan's rules.

- Adder circuits are the basic building blocks of the processor; the half-adder takes two inputs and outputs the sum and carry. A full adder is made from two half adders and an OR gate and can output the sum and carry for three inputs.
- A flip-flop can store one item of data (0 or 1). Flip-flop circuits are combined to make a range of other flip-flop circuits such as the D-Type flip-flop. The D-type flip-flop delays a signal by exactly one clock pulse. It has two inputs – data and a clock – and outputs the data and the inverse of the data.

15 Databases

A **database** is a **structured persistent** store of data. Databases are stored on the secondary storage devices of a computer system.

> **Database** A structured store of data, organised so that it can easily be accessed, managed and updated.
>
> **Structured** The data is organised in a logical way to facilitate processing.
>
> **Persistent** The data remains for as long as is required.

Benefits of databases

Most computer systems make use of databases. This is because they make it convenient and fast to:
- access data
- update data
- search for data
- present data in a usable way.

Now test yourself

1 A car contains many computer systems. Identify at least three and, for each, list possible databases that they might need to access at some point in their working lives.

Answers on page 155

Databases:
- provide security
- provide automatic backup
- enforce data integrity rules
- control data redundancy
- provide users with controlled access to data they need.

Data security is keeping data safe, from:
- accidental or deliberate loss
- malicious access.

An important aspect of data security is control over who has access to it and what they are permitted to do, such as view or change the data.

To back up means to keep additional copies of data somewhere other than at the working location. Nowadays that usually means in the cloud.

Data integrity is the state of data being:
- as intended
- accurate.

Data integrity is enhanced by:
- designing the database sensibly in the first place
- using validation techniques to reduce the likelihood of bad data being entered in the first place.

Files

Files are data stores on a computer's secondary storage medium. Files:
- have names
- are stores of binary data.

Files may be unstructured data streams such as:
- a program
- a word-processed document
- an image
- music.

Database files are **structured data**. The data is organised in a planned and predictable way. Databases are made from units called 'records'. Each record is composed of sub-units called 'fields'.

Serial file:

field	name	dob	name	dob	name	dob	name	dob
data	Tristan	12/3/87	Isolde	13/5/90	Mark	21/1/70	Brangane	24/6/87

Sequential file: In this file, the names are arranged in alphabetical order:

field	name	dob	name	dob	name	dob	name	dob
data	Brangane	24/6/87	Isolde	13/5/90	Mark	21/1/70	Tristan	12/3/87

Now test yourself

2 Give an example of where a serial file is an appropriate way to store data.
3 Give an example of where a sequential file is an appropriate way to store data.

Answers on page 155

Indexing

Most databases make use of indexes to speed up searches. They are just like indexes in a book. The software first searches for the start of the right section (like a book chapter), then directs the search to the right part of the main data store. After that, a sequential search can look for the item in a reduced part of the data store.

Index file			Data file	
Category	Data file start position		Position	Data
A	1		1	Abbott
B	10		2	Abby
C	20		3	Abercrombie
D	45		4	Agamemnon
E	80		5	Albemarle
			6	Alvarez
			7	Angstrom
			8	Anthracite
			9	Avery
			10	Baird
			11	Barr
			12	Barry
			13	Barton
			14	Brennan
			15	Buckley
			16	Bullock
			17	Bush

Figure 15.1 Sequential files can be searched more quickly

Structured data Organised in a planned and predictable way for ease of processing.

Serial files Stores of similarly structured records, set out one after another.

Sequential files Serial files but stored in some order, usually based on the alphabetical or numerical order of some field.

Revision activity

Try writing code to demonstrate processes, even simple ones. This will help you to remember more and enable you to apply your knowledge in new situations.

Large databases have multiple indexes. These can look for subsections within sections. They can also search on various criteria.

Now test yourself

TESTED ☐

4 How can a credit card company quickly find your details when you enquire, even if you have forgotten your card number?

Answer on page 155

When an indexed database is updated, its associated indexes have to be updated along with the data. This can slow processing down.

Now test yourself

TESTED ☐

5 What is a database?
6 What are the individual components of a database?
7 What is meant by structured data?

Answers on page 155

Flat-file databases

Simple databases can be made as lists in a table, like in a spreadsheet. They are called flat-file databases. These are of limited use. They are fine for small amounts of data but are cumbersome to update. They do not support complex applications. They are also prone to **data redundancy**.

Data redundancy is a bad thing because when updates occur, all the instances of a data item must be changed. This leads to errors. Also, it wastes storage space. It is much better to have just one copy of all data items so that users always get to see the one updated copy.

Relational databases should be designed to reduce data redundancy. The process of **normalisation** is intended to assist this process.

Separating data from applications

In the past, software was written specially to handle a particular database. This led to problems when the data structures had to be changed. The software often had to be redesigned from scratch.

Most database systems now are controlled at the physical data level by general purpose software called database management systems that look after safety-related issues such as security and integrity. The applications work through these, thereby ensuring data safety as well as reducing the workload of the applications programmers.

Fixed and variable length fields

Some databases store only as much data as is needed, so that 'Fred' takes four bytes and 'Jennifer' takes eight bytes. This method is called using variable length fields. This is obviously as economical as possible. But, it makes processing more difficult. Finding a particular record requires checking all the preceding entries sequentially.

> **Data redundancy** The unnecessary duplication of data in a database. When updates occur, all the instances of a data item must be changed. This leads to errors and also wastes storage space.
>
> **Normalisation** Organising the attributes and relations of a relational database to minimise data redundancy.

A more common method is to reserve a suitable amount of space in a file and any unused bytes are padded with a character such as a space. This is less space efficient but makes processing more straightforward because bytes can be counted to reach the desired point.

| S | m | i | t | h | | | | | | | | | | | | |

Hashing

Hashing is a method of transforming a string of characters in a record into a shortened form that can be used as a disk address. This shortened form (has value) can be used to access a record from a database more quickly than by using the complete original string.

Typically, multiple records can usually produce some hash values that are the same. In this case, the data is located in the next available space (or block) on the storage medium, so some serial searching may be necessary.

Now test yourself

TESTED

8 What is a flat-file database?
9 Give one example of a situation that could sensibly make use of a flat-file database.
10 What is the difference between fixed and variable length fields?
11 Explain the advantage of using fixed length fields.

Answers on page 155

Relational databases

REVISED

There are various models of database, such as hierarchical, network and relational. Relational is the most common database model.

Relational databases are:
- based on tables (also known as relations)
- tables are linked: primary keys to foreign keys
- each table is based on a real–life entity
- an entity is anything about which we store data, for example customer, invoice, stock item
- a table consists of tuples (equivalent to records).

A tuple is information about one instance of an entity, for example all we need to know about a customer called Fred, or another customer.

An entity has attributes. These are characteristics of the entity, for example `customer_name`, `student_id`, `subject_level`.

Attributes become fields in a table. In a table, fields are often referred to as columns and records as rows.
- Relational databases use fixed length fields.
- Each column contains data of just one type.
- There is no rule about the order of rows in a table. When order is required, indexes are added.
- There is no rule about the order of columns.
- No two rows can be identical.
- One column or combination of columns must be able to make each row unique. This column or combination is called the primary key.
- A primary key is used to link a table to the foreign keys of other tables.

Example

Here is part of a data table. It is designed to store details of hotel-room bookings. It shows three rows and four columns.

room_number	date	room_type	customer_ref
101	21/03/2015	double	26335
310	22/03/2015	single	45335
250	23/03/2015	double	36587

Note that a combination of room number and date is sufficient to make a primary key field. Many tables make use of a special reference such as student_number to produce a key field.

The tables of a relational database are linked through relationships. Relationships are produced by having repeated fields. A field repeated from another table is called a foreign key.

Example

Here, the field customer_ref forms the primary key in tblCustomer, but is a foreign key in tblRoomBooking. It allows a relationship to link the tables.

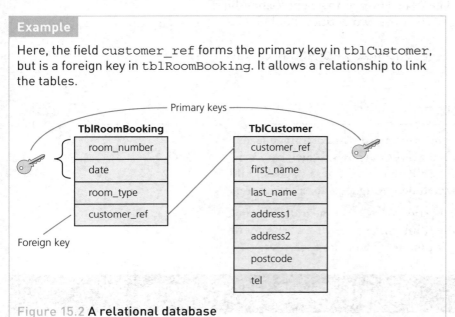

Figure 15.2 **A relational database**

Secondary keys are not necessarily unique data items but can be useful for quick searching.

Now test yourself

TESTED ☐

12 What order is used to store rows in a table in a relational database?
13 What is a primary key?
14 State two reasons why primary keys are necessary.
15 A data table stores the following fields about insurance policies:
  (a) policy number
  (b) owner reference number
  (c) sum assured
  (d) type of policy
  (e) renewal date.
  Which of these fields would be usable as a primary key in this table? Why?

Answers on page 155

Entity relationship modelling

REVISED

When planning a database, it necessary to design the tables in such way as to reduce data redundancy. Basically, this is an attempt to make all the data in each table relate to just one entity. There are processes to go through to ensure this. These processes are called 'normalisation'. Normalisation can be helped by making an **entity relation diagram (ERD)**. Typically, ERDs use 'crow's feet' diagrams to show how entities, and hence tables, are laid out.

> **ERD (Entity Relationship Diagram)** A data modelling technique used to define a relational database.

Figure 15.3 Representing a data model with one-to-many relationships

One prong means one, three prongs means many. In this diagram:
- One customer can place many orders.
- Each order can have many items.

Tables in relational databases should be related by one-to-many relationships.
- A one-to-one relationship suggests that the two entities should be in the same table.
- A many-to-many relationship suggests the need for at least one more table to separate entities.

Database normalisation

REVISED

There are various stages in the normalisation process. Each stage leads to a state known as a normal form. For most purposes, stages 1 to 3 are sufficient. They are known as 1NF, 2NF and 3NF. These stages should be worked through in succession when designing a database structure.

For example, if we consider this collection of data about students from a school or college, we might initially think that Student_number will make a good primary key because it uniquely identifies each row.

Student_number	SName	Street_address	City	Postcode	Subject_number	Subject_taken
1456	Jones A.	12 Queen Street	Inverness	IV3 5LH	12	Computing
					15	Biology
					16	Greek
					11	Maths
1654	Patel R.	6 High Street	Milton Keynes	MK44 1BY	15	Biology
					19	French
					16	Greek
1543	Patel S.	6 High Street	Milton Keynes	MK44 1BY	14	Physics
					17	German
					16	Greek

Already you will see that this will be hard to process. Each student has many subjects. Suppose you needed to write an application to find all the students studying Greek. This would be excessively complex.

A rule is that multiple values in one row are not allowed.

This data is not normalised yet. It is in 0NF. We need to make some changes.

First normal form (1NF)

Remove duplicate values. We do this by creating separate rows for each instance of a subject.

We get:

Student_ number	SName	Street_ address	City	Postcode	Subject_ number	Subject_taken
1456	Jones A.	12 Queen Street	Inverness	IV3 5LH	12	Computing
1456	Jones A.	12 Queen Street	Inverness	IV3 5LH	15	Biology
1456	Jones A.	12 Queen Street	Inverness	IV3 5LH	16	Greek
1456	Jones A.	12 Queen Street	Inverness	IV3 5LH	11	Maths
1654	Patel R.	6 High Street	Milton Keynes	MK44 1BY	15	Biology
1654	Patel R.	6 High Street	Milton Keynes	MK44 1BY	19	French
1654	Patel R.	6 High Street	Milton Keynes	MK44 1BY	16	Greek
1543	Patel S.	6 High Street	Milton Keynes	MK44 1BY	14	Physics
1543	Patel S.	6 High Street	Milton Keynes	MK44 1BY	17	German
1543	Patel S.	6 High Street	Milton Keynes	MK44 1BY	16	Greek

We need a primary key. We cannot use Student_number because it is not unique for each row any more.

● We can make a composite primary key by combining Student_ number with Subject_number. For example, 1456:16 identifies Jones taking Greek and no other row.

The table is now in 1NF.

Now test yourself

TESTED

16 Why is a composite primary key possible for this table?
17 Suggest another way to give this table a primary key.

Answers on page 155

Second normal form (2NF)

There is still redundant data in this table. Names and subjects are needlessly repeated.

● Take the table that is in 1NF.
● Remove data sets that occur in multiple rows. Place them in a new table.
● Create relationships between tables through foreign keys.

We then get:

Table Students

Student_ number	SName	Street_address	City	Postcode
1456	Jones A.	12 Queen Street	Inverness	IV3 5LH
1654	Patel R.	6 High Street	Milton Keynes	MK44 1BY
1543	Patel S.	6 High Street	Milton Keynes	MK44 1BY

Student_number can be the primary key.

This table stores the contact information for each student with no redundancy.

We also need:

Table Subject entry

Student_ number	SName	Subject_ number	Subject_taken
1456	Jones A.	12	Computing
1456	Jones A.	15	Biology
1456	Jones A.	16	Greek
1456	Jones A.	11	Maths
1654	Patel R.	15	Biology
1654	Patel R.	19	French
1654	Patel R.	16	Greek
1543	Patel S.	14	Physics
1543	Patel S.	17	German
1543	Patel S.	16	Greek

A candidate key for this would be a combination of Student_number and Subject_number.

With the data arranged like this, there will be no update anomalies because each row can be identified uniquely by this composite key.

Third normal form (3NF)

However, there is still some redundancy in this arrangement. Names and subjects are repeated. Not all the details in these tables are dependent upon the whole of the primary key. For example, French is only dependent on `Subject_number`, not `Student_number`. We need to take normalisation a step further.

● Remove columns that are not dependent on the primary key.

This leads to 3NF.

Table Student entry

Student_number	Subject_ number
1456	12
1456	15
1456	16
1456	11
1654	15
1654	19
1654	16
1543	14
1543	17
1543	16

`Student_number` and `Subject_number` can be a composite primary key. Alternatively, you could create a new column called `Entry_number`.

We link this to a new subject table.

Table Subject

Subject_ number	Subject_name
12	Computing
15	Biology
16	Greek
11	Maths
19	French
14	Physics
17	German

`Subject_number` can be the primary key.

> **Exam tip**
>
> To get to 3NF, check that each non-key column is dependent on the key, the whole key and nothing but the key!

TESTED ☐

Now test yourself

18 Here is a preliminary design for a database to store stock details and handle orders in a shop.
```
stock_number, stock_name, number_in_stock,
supplier ref, supplier_name, supplier_email,
order_number, order_date, order_quantity
```
Normalise this database into 3NF.

Answer on page 156

The database management system (DBMS)

REVISED ☐

The database management system (DBMS) is software that handles the data that is stored in secondary storage. It acts as an intermediary between the applications and the data.

Exam tip

Remember, the application is the software that the users work with. It might be an application to generate exam entries or send out fee demands. Whatever it is, it has to work through the DBMS.

The DBMS provides:
- security
- backup functionality
- index updating
- enforcement of **referential integrity**
- facilities to update and interrogate the database.

> **Referential integrity** The state of a database being consistent. For example, you cannot delete a record if it is linked to a record in another table.

Database views

REVISED ☐

There are three main layers of a database.
1 **Physical view:** the data that is written to storage. The 0s and 1s on disk.
2 **Logical view:** the organisation of the tables, queries and reports.
3 **User view:** the interface that allows the user to interact with the database.

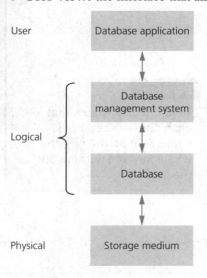

Figure 15.4 Views of a database

ACID rules

ACID rules are rules that protect the integrity of a database.

1 Atomicity: A change is performed or not performed. Half-finished changes must not be saved.

2 Consistency: Any change must retain the overall state of the database, for example money out of one account must be balanced by money into another.

3 Isolation: A **transaction** must not be able to be interrupted by a different transaction. A transaction is locked until the change is committed then it is released.

4 Durability: Changes must be written to storage in order to preserve them.

> **Transaction** A change in a database.

Query language

DBMSs provide a means of manipulating and querying the database. This includes the actions of setting them up and changing their structure. Some DBMSs provide a graphical interface to do this called query by example (QBE). This can be handy but it does not give such total control as a query language.

Query languages provide a means of handling a database by writing commands which can be grouped into scripts. This allows a greater degree of control than using QBE.

Structured query language (SQL) is a commonly used query language. There are many variants of this with slightly differing syntax. The following show examples from the popular DBMS MySQL.

Examples of MySQL

You can do pretty well anything to and with a database with MySQL or other query language.

You can start a new database.

```
mysql> CREATE DATABASE VEGETABLES;
```

Query OK, 1 row affected (0.00 sec)

Look to see that it is there with:

```
mysql> SHOW DATABASES;
+----------------------------+
| Database                   |
+----------------------------+
| information_schema         |
| OCR                        |
| VEGETABLES                 |
| exam                       |
| example                    |
| invoices                   |
| menagerie                  |
| mysql                      |
| ocr                        |
| origin                     |
| performance_schema         |
+----------------------------+
```

11 rows in set (0.00 sec)

> **Revision activity**
>
> To understand databases properly, you must have experience of creating, amending and interrogating one and it should have at least three linked tables and one or two queries.
>
> Try setting up the queries in QBE (Query By Example) then flipping across to the SQL view. Try making changes in one view then seeing the effects in the other.
>
> You can do this quite easily by using one of the generic tools such as MS Access or Libre Office Base.
>
> This may take some time to get right but it is essential practice.
>
> If you have the time, you should also try doing the same from scratch in a purely SQL environment. This is particularly informative if you have MySQL available on a Linux system.

Make a table called 'green' for green vegetables, with three columns, specify the field names and data types at the same time:

```
mysql> CREATE TABLE IF NOT EXISTS green (name TEXT,
price _ per _ kg INT, origin _ code INT);
```

Check that it is there with DESCRIBE:

```
mysql> DESCRIBE green;

+----------------+--------+------+-----+----------+--------+
| Field          | Type   | Null | Key | Default  | Extra  |
+----------------+--------+------+-----+----------+--------+
| name           | text   | YES  |     | NULL     |        |
| price_per_kg   | int(11)| YES  |     | NULL     |        |
| origin_code    | int(11)| YES  |     | NULL     |        |
+----------------+--------+------+-----+----------+--------+
```

3 rows in set (0.00 sec)

Now add some data:

```
mysql> INSERT INTO green (name, price _ per _ kg,
origin _ code) VALUES ("cabbage", 1,1), ("leeks", 2,1),
("sprouts",3,2);
```

Query OK, 3 rows affected (0.04 sec)

```
Display it all with SELECT: (* means everything)

mysql> SELECT * from green;
+----------+--------------+--------------+
| name     | price_per_kg | origin_code  |
+----------+--------------+--------------+
| cabbage  |            1 |            1 |
| leeks    |            2 |            1 |
| sprouts  |            3 |            2 |
+----------+--------------+--------------+
```

3 rows in set (0.00 sec)

Make a table to store country-of-origin details:

```
mysql> CREATE TABLE IF NOT EXISTS origin (origin_code
INT,country_name TEXT);
```

Add data:

```
mysql> INSERT INTO origin (origin_code,country_name)
VALUES (1,"France"), (2,"UK");
```

Query OK, 2 rows affected (0.04 sec)

Check that it's there with a SELECT * statement.

Other actions that can be performed with SQL.

DELETE removes data, for example:

```
DELETE FROM green WHERE name="leeks";
```

DROP can be used to remove database components.

ALTER TABLE used with DROP can remove a column, for example:

```
ALTER TABLE green DROP COLUMN name;
```

This removes the entire column called 'name'.

You can DROP indexes, tables and whole databases too.

JOIN is used to combine data from two or more tables. So if you want to show the country of origin of the vegetables, you JOIN the two tables on the field origin_code.

```
mysql> SELECT green.name,
-> origin.country _ name
-> FROM
-> green
-> JOIN origin
-> ON green.origin _ code=origin.origin _ code;
```

This displays the vegetables together with the correct country of origin.

```
+---------+--------------+
| name    | country_name |
+---------+--------------+
| cabbage | France       |
| leeks   | France       |
| sprouts | UK           |
+---------+--------------+
```

3 rows in set (0.00 sec)

Revision activity

Get hold of MySQL. There are free downloads for all platforms. Try a few simple commands and, if you have time, combine some to form scripts.

Working at the command line will teach you more than just looking up the SQL equivalents to QBE generated by programs such as MS Access.

Exam tip

If you practise SQL statements and scripts, stick to just one version. The various versions of SQL are NOT compatible.

Exam practice

1 A veterinary practice needs a database to administer its clients and their animals, plus details of consultations and treatments. The vets also want to send out reminders to clients by text message about when their pets' vaccinations and treatments are due.
   (a) Identify the data items that will be needed in order to fulfil these requirements. [6]
   (b) Produce a relational database structure, normalised to 3NF, that could be used in this situation. [6]
   (c) Produce an SQL statement that would produce a list of animals that need their flea treatments for a particular day. [6]
2 Explain the difference between data redundancy and data integrity. [4]
3 (a) Explain the meaning of referential integrity. [2]
   (b) Illustrate the concept of referential integrity with an example. [2]
4 (a) In terms of a database, explain the term transaction. [2]
   (b) Explain where record locking might be needed in the performance of a database transaction. [2]
5 Write an algorithm for adding a record to a serial file. [4]
6 Write an algorithm for adding a record to a sequential file. [4]

Answers on page 166

Summary

- A database is a structured persistent store of data on a computer system.
- Databases underpin or support most computer applications, even when not immediately apparent.
- Databases make data accessible and allow its flexible use as well as providing important security features.
- Databases come in various forms. Some are simple serial or sequential files. Some simple ones, called 'flat-file database's, are just one table.
- Simple database implementations are limited in their flexibility and usefulness.
- Most are more structured and organised than that to allow easier and more reliable processing.
- Speed of access is an issue with databases. This is usually optimised by the use of indexes that use pointers to locate and retrieve data directly from secondary storage.
- Most databases are administered by software called a 'database management system' (DBMS). This handles the low-level functionality and provides security features. Applications are written to work through the DBMS to access the data in whatever way is required for some particular purpose such as making bookings or taking orders online.
- Databases are mostly built on one of a small number of typical models, the most common being the relational model.
- The relational model stores data in linked tables, where each table holds data about a real-life entity.
- Each table consists of records that are themselves made up from fields.
- Each table has a primary key to identify each record uniquely.
- Each record in a table is constructed in exactly the same way, which facilitates easy and ordered processing.
- There are rules for the construction of relational databases that ensure that data is ordered sensibly and that redundancy is avoided. These rules are implemented in a process called 'normalisation' – not to be confused with normalisation of floating point numbers.
- Redundant data is data that is needlessly repeated and can lead to inconsistent updates.
- ACID rules are applied by the DBMS to avoid update problems.
- Databases are usually managed by a DBMS query language such as MySQL.
- Query languages provide tools to allow the creation, update and interrogation of a database.

16 Data transmission

Most computers are connected in some way. This has become possible and useful because:
- digital signals can be transmitted accurately
- common standards have increasingly been adopted.

Organisations and private individuals need networks. Networks allow:
- sharing of data
- collaborative working
- communication.

Networks

REVISED

A network is an interconnected set of devices. Each device is referred to as a node. Nowadays, most computing devices are connected to many networks via the internet.

Private networks

Most organisations have private networks, although increasingly networking is done online.

Advantages of private networks are:
- the institution controls security
- security issues typically involve who is allowed what privileges
- software is totally under the institution's control
- the institution is not reliant on someone else providing reliability.

Disadvantages of private networks include:
- they need specialised staff
- a need to make own arrangements about security and backups.

Precautions that can be taken against loss of data or functionality include:
- redundancy – duplicate servers and other equipment
- backup regime
- failover systems – automatic transfer to backup system in the event of failure
- disaster recovery plan – processes, procedures and personnel responsibilities in the event of a major incident.

Hardware

REVISED

Network interface card/controller
- Receives and sends electrical signals.

A Level only

Router
- Device to connect networks.
- Receives and forwards data packets.
- Directs packets to next device. Uses a table or an algorithm to decide the route.

MAC address
- 48-bit identifier.
- Permanently added to a device by the manufacturer.
- Human readable groups of 6 bytes (octets).
- Example: 08:01:27:0E:25:B8.

Switches

- Devices to connect other devices on networks.
- Use packet switching to send data to specific destinations making use of hardware addresses.
- Operate at level 2 or 3 of the OSI model (see page 124).

Hubs

- Connect nodes together by broadcasting a signal to all possible destinations.
- The correct destination will accept the signal.

Wireless access points

- Most devices can use wireless to connect to a WiFi network.
- Can connect from distances of up to about 100 metres.

Transmission media

- Most networks use cables to connect the nodes. These can be:
  - copper conductors – fairly cheap to implement
  - fibre optic – a greater data capacity than copper wire.
- Increasingly, wireless is used for part of the network. This allows great flexibility but is slower than physical cable and poses different security threats.

Security issues

- Eavesdropping by intercepting the wireless signals.
- Reduce risk by:
  - hiding SSID (service set identifier) – but this limits usefulness to new users
  - encryption – most use WPA and WPA2, which use once-only encryption keys
  - limiting access – only allow access to known MAC addresses.

Classification of networks

REVISED

Topology

Topology refers to the layout of a network; how the nodes are connected. There are three that you need to know about:

Bus

- Attaches nodes along a common backbone.
- Cheap to implement, but if there is a problem with the backbone the whole network fails.
- It is not used much these days.

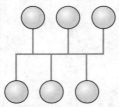

Figure 16.1 Bus network layout

Ring

- The nodes are attached to a circular backbone.
- Data **frames** are sent in one direction. They pass each node and are collected by whichever node is specified by the address data in the frame.

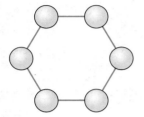

Figure 16.2 Ring network layout

> **Frame** A unit of data sent on a network. Its composition is dependent on the protocol used.

Star

- By far the most common topology.
- Relatively cheap to implement and robust because each node has a separate connection to a switch.
- Cable failures do not affect the whole network.

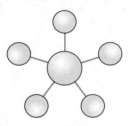

Figure 16.3 Star network layout

Extent

There are so many network types that classifications become blurred, but during the exam there are certain types that can be asked about.

LAN

- Local area network.
- Network is confined to one location, such as a building or a campus.
- Infrastructure is maintained by the organisation that owns it.

WAN

- Wide area network.
- Covers a large geographical area.
- Makes use of communication providers such as BT.
- Internet is a WAN but a special case because of its multiplicity of users.

SAN

- Storage area network.
- Linked servers that provide large scale storage for data centres.

MAN

- Metropolitan area network.
- A city-wide network.

PAN

- Personal area network.
- Many individuals have networks in their homes. These are often further enhanced by cloud connections.

Networks are everywhere. Cars increasingly have their own networks, with many interconnected processors that also access the internet.

Increasingly these terms are becoming less meaningful because of the wide variety of ways to connect devices over long and short distances.

Now test yourself   TESTED

1 List the differences between a LAN and a WAN.

Answers on page 156

Network models   REVISED

Client–server

Most networks are constructed on the client–server model. This means that one, or usually many, high end computers act as servers. Servers provide services to the users, or clients. Services include:
- file storage and access
- printing
- internet access
- security features such as logins and audit trails.

Client–server is usually the favoured model because:
- client computers need not be expensive and powerful
- it is easier to make data and often software accessible from anywhere in the network
- banks of servers can be combined to make best use of their potential
- separate functionality can be devolved to virtual servers or physical servers.

Peer-to-peer

With peer-to-peer, each computer has an equal status. It is generally a cheap and not very common way of implementing a network but it is a popular means on the internet to pass files between users without the need to go through servers. Peer-to-peer is a useful way to make use of distributed computing to promote collaborative working.

The cloud

This is a fairly new extension to networking. It entails having data and often software stored remotely on servers maintained by various providers.

Its benefits to individuals as well as organisations include:
- less need to buy and upgrade software
- backing up is dealt with by the provider
- data is accessible anywhere.

Some disadvantages are that users rely on someone else
- to keep their data safe
- to ensure the availability of services.

> **Revision activity**
>
> Research some cloud providers. Find out what services they provide and what provisions they make or claim to make regarding the security of stored data.
>
> Which ones also provide remotely accessible software?
>
> How do various cloud providers differ in what they charge for their services?

Layering

Layering is the principle of dividing a complex system into separate slices of functionality. It is common in computing systems as well as other aspects of life such as engineering.

Layering is an **abstraction**; a way of looking at reality.

Layering allows the creation and maintenance of parts of a system without having to take the whole system into account.

Each layer communicates only with adjacent layers. This simplifies interfacing.

Layering can be found in operating systems and databases as well as networking.

Start by considering a networking system with three layers. In reality, there will be more than this.

Consider these three questions:
1 What is being communicated?
2 Where is it being sent?
3 How will it get there?

Each of these aspects can be considered separately.

These three layers can be named:
1 **Application layer:** This collects and disseminates data. Think about a normal human–machine interface. It needs to collect data in a standard way and give information back in a way that the user (human or machine) requires.
2 **Network layer:** This doesn't care about what the data is. It is only concerned about how to get the data from A to B.
3 **Physical layer:** This doesn't care about routing. It is only concerned with transmitting signals. It's about cables, hardware and wireless.

> **Abstraction** A process of solving problems by identifying common patterns in real situations.

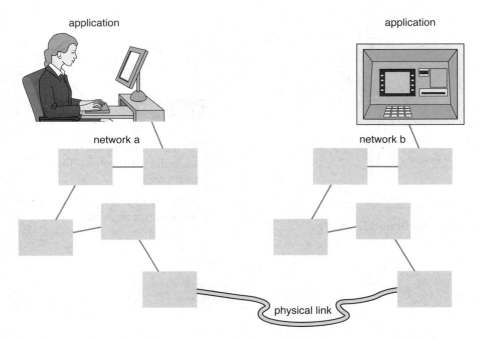

Figure 16.4 A simple three-layer network model; in this case, an ATM is being administered remotely by bank staff

Open systems interconnection (OSI)

Three layers is too crude to get the best out of layering. In reality there will be more. The OSI model specifies seven layers. Levels close to the human user are high. The top level is level 7. Layers close to the devices and connecting equipment are low.

Layer	Name	Purpose
7	Application	The layer closest to the user. Collects or delivers data and passes it to and from the presentation layer.
6	Presentation	Looks after any conversions between data as sent on the network and data as it is needed by the applications. May involve encryption/decryption operations.
5	Session	Looks after starting, managing and terminating connection sessions. Provides simplex, half-duplex and full duplex operation.
4	Transport	Concerned with keeping track of segments of a network, checking successful transmission and packetisation, for example TCP.
3	Network	Transmission of data packets, routing.
2	Data link	Control of access, error detection and correction.
1	Physical	Network devices and transmission media.

Messages pass from a sender through such a network from high to low, then back through the layers low to high to reach the receiver.

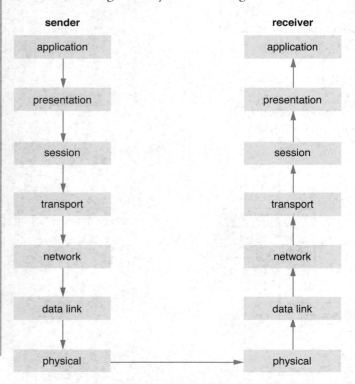

Figure 16.5 An open systems interconnection (OSI) model

Exam tips

Try to learn the OSI sequence. There are some useful mnemonics for this – look them up!

Also, try to learn the basics of what happens at each layer.

Protocols

REVISED

These are rules and standards that govern data transmission. They ensure that devices can talk to each other.

The TCP/IP stack

Transmission control protocol/internet protocol (TCP/IP) is the most common set of protocols. It is used to bring order to the internet as well as many private networks. It covers:

● data formatting
● routing
● addressing.

TCP/IP has four layers of abstraction.

Layer	Purpose
Application	Concerned with production and reception of data. Packages data and passes it to the transport layer.
Transport	Concerned with making and breaking connections via routers.
Internet	Concerned with providing links across different network types. Essential feature of the internet that allows interoperability between all connected systems.
Link	Passes data to the physical network. It can work with any media such as copper wire, optical fibre and wireless.

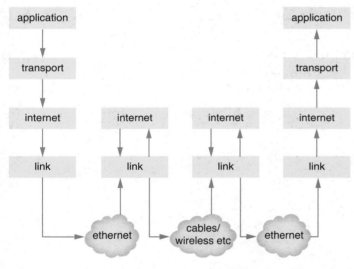

Figure 16.6 The four TCP/IP layers in the practical operation of the internet

Now test yourself

TESTED

2 What is the OSI network model?
3 Explain the usefulness of designing networks in layers.
4 Explain the relationship between the TCP/IP link layer and the transmission media.

Answers on page 156

Circuit switching

This is the establishment of a physical connection between two communicating entities.
● It provides an exclusive dedicated channel.
● The channel remains open for the duration of the communication session.

Circuit switching has three phases:
1 connection established
2 Data transferred
3 Connection released.

Circuit switching ties up a link so that when in use, other entities cannot use it.

It is suitable when there is a need for intensive data transfer, for example batch processing a data stream.

In reality, modern fast broadband transmissions make circuit switching less important.

Packet switching

Most networks make use of packet switching. Packet switching divides a message into data units called packets. A packet of data is a standard unit, whose makeup is decided by the network protocol.

Typically a data packet contains the following data items:

Header				Payload	Trailer	
source address	destination address	packet sequence number	protocol	data	checksum	end of packet marker

Packets are sent across a network by whichever routes are available or most efficient. The parts of a message may be passed by many different routes and combined at the receiving end. Terminals communicate with each other across connected routers.

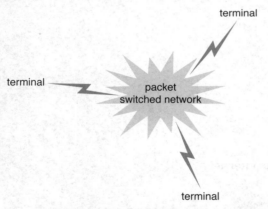

Figure 16.7 Concept of a packet-switched network

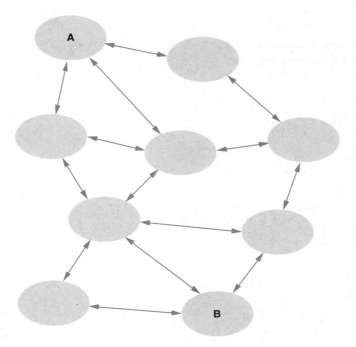

Figure 16.8 Sending a message from A to B; note that multiple routers allow many possible pathways

Packet switching helps to make the internet reliable. If one route is unavailable, there are always others. This is one of many examples of how redundancy can boost reliability.

IP addressing

Each node on the internet has an IP (internet protocol) address. This ensures that messages get to where they are intended.

An IP address is composed of a series of binary numbers, normally displayed in decimal or hex. IP Version 4 (IPv4) uses four octets, for example 194.83.249.5. This gives 4,294,967,296 IP addresses.

> **Revision activity**
>
> Use a tracer program to get a feel for the jumps made by packets from one resource to another on the internet.

Now test yourself

TESTED ☐

5 What is an octet?

Answer on page 156

Internet Protocol Version 6 (IPv6) uses more bytes, for example 2001:db8:0:1234:10:567:12:11. This provides about 340 trillion trillion trillion IP addresses.

IP addresses can be static; that is, they are assigned by an administrator.

To conserve IP addresses, they are often assigned dynamically, to allow reuse. This is called DHCP (dynamic host configuration protocol).

Networks often have their own subnet addresses, again to conserve addresses. The router connecting to the outside world has one and the clients inside the LAN have their own.

DNS (domain name system)

We request resources on the internet by asking for a named address, like hodder.co.uk. The named address is called its URL (uniform resource locator).

This is easier to remember than 69.172.201.167.

Domain names are constructed from a hierarchy.

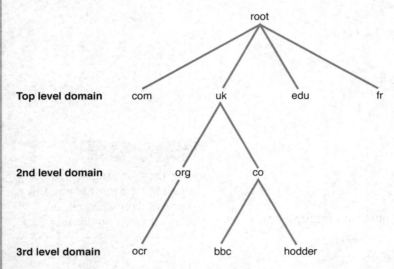

Figure 16.9 **A hierarchical naming system**

Now test yourself TESTED ☐

6 Produce a DNS hierarchy diagram that would accommodate the following URLs:
   (a) www.stanford.edu/
   (b) www.princeton.edu/
   (c) www.cmu.edu/
   (d) www.cam.ac.uk/
   (e) www.worcester.ac.uk/

Answers on page 156

Domain names are looked up on domain name servers. These translate URLs into IP addresses.

A Level only

Security/threats

REVISED ☐

Networks pose security problems. There are many potential entry points.

Authentication

Most networks are protected by users having a username and password. These can be cracked quite easily by simple methods such as asking someone for them or simply guessing. A crude but effective form of guessing uses software where all possible combinations are tried one after another. This is called a brute force attack.

As hackers find new ways to subvert security systems, new ways of improving security are invented. Access to many networks now requires:
- multiple credentials
- smart cards
- biometric information such as fingerprints or iris scans.

7 Describe a few networks or online resources that require more sophisticated authentication than a simple user id and password.

Answers on page 156

Firewalls

Firewalls are various combinations of hardware and software that can isolate a network from the outside world. They are configurable to allow or deny access to certain addresses or certain types of data.

Proxies

These are computers that are interposed between a network and a remote resource. They can react in a more sophisticated way to control input to and output from a network.

Encryption

Most network traffic is encrypted; that is, made unintelligible to unauthorised individuals.

Data is encrypted using:
● an algorithm and
● a key.

The key is needed by both the sender to encrypt and the receiver to decrypt a message.

The algorithm uses the key to generate an encrypted message.

The bigger the key, the more secure is the encryption.

A common method is to use two keys such as the public/private key method. This is an example of **asymmetric key encryption**.

> **Asymmetric key encryption**
> One key is publicly available. It is used to encrypt a message. A secret private key is linked to this and is required to decrypt the message. Only the holder of the paired private key can decrypt.

A Level only

Exam practice

1 Describe two methods of keeping a network secure from online hackers. [4]
2 (a) Explain the benefits of using layers as a basis for designing a network. [4]
  (b) Describe the interactions between layers 1 and 2 of the OSI model. [2]
  (c) Explain the differences between OSI and TCP/IP network approaches. [6]
  (d) Explain why network layering can be described as an abstraction. [2]
3 Explain the purpose of a router in a network. [2]
4 Explain what a network protocol is. [3]
5 Explain the concept of packet switching and how it differs from circuit switching. [6]
6 Describe the steps taken to send a message from Bob to Alice using asymmetric key encryption. [6]

Answers on page 167

Summary

- Most computers are connected to others in some way. The reliable and cheap nature of digital signals makes this a relatively easy thing to do in concept and has led to the widespread use of computer networks.
- There are numerous advantages to networking computers, such as sharing data and work streams; communication; and data storage. Many large organisations have their own private networks to facilitate their business.
- Networks have vulnerabilities. Data on the move can be intercepted and stolen. Various security measures attempt to reduce this risk, such as firewalls, encryption and proxy servers.
- Important data is backed up in case of loss.
- There is fairly standard hardware that is used to connect devices on a network, such as routers, switches, hubs, NICs (network interface cards/controllers) and various forms of cabling or wireless equipment. Wireless networks have additional vulnerabilities because of the ease with which their signals can be intercepted.
- Data is sent to its destination on a network using the address of the intended receiving device. This address is stored in the hardware of each device and is called the 'MAC address'.
- The physical layout of a network is called its 'topology'.
- The extent of a network is often described by a three-letter acronym, such as LAN or WAN. You should know the differences between the common ones.
- Most private networks are built on the client–server model, where one or more high-end machine controls the network functionality. Peer-to-peer networks are less common and all computers on such a network have equal status. This is a useful concept for some file-sharing activities on the internet.
- Most users these days make use of the cloud, which is an abstraction referring to hardware and services provided remotely.
- Networks are built using the abstraction of layering. Layering is a concept whereby the whole system is divided into 'layers' of functionality that communicate only with adjacent layers.
- Layering is a common concept in computing, and indeed beyond. It simplifies the development and maintenance of complex systems.
- You should have a good understanding of the OSI and TCP/IP layer models and how they relate to each other.
- Networks use protocols or rules and standards to ensure connectivity.
- Most modern networks use packet switching, where messages are divided into sections that then travel by various routes to their destination.
- Packet switching is one reason why the internet is so reliable. If one section is not working, another can be used.
- The nature and behaviour of packets is just one aspect of a network protocol.
- Algorithms such as Dijkstra's shortest-path algorithm are used to optimise the pathways taken by data packets across a network.
- The internet uses IP addressing to identify nodes (devices), followed at the end by the use of MAC addresses. IP addressing assigns a different number to each device. The IP address can in most cases be reassigned as needed, using DHCP (dynamic host configuration protocol).
- IP addresses are often replaced by user-friendly URL addresses for ease of understanding. DNS servers do the conversions.

17 The internet

Our world has been changed by the internet in a very short period of time. Humanity is still adjusting to it and finding new uses for it.

The internet is:
- a network of networks
- an infrastructure – it is not content; it is not the world wide web
- reliable – note redundancy and the simplicity of binary data representation
- independent of computer platforms – note the use of protocols
- cheap to use – sending signals does not require a lot of power
- fast – bandwidth is increasing all the time.

Uses

REVISED

The internet has many uses already. More are being invented all the time. Principal examples include:

Communication

- Human communication via the internet ranges from emails to chat sessions, to VoIP (Voice over Internet Protocol), for example Skype.
- Devices can be controlled by signals sent over the internet.

Information

- Human knowledge is now saved on internet-connected servers as a matter of routine.
- This makes it easily and quickly accessible and searchable.

Entertainment

There is a huge supply of entertainment available online such as:
- games
- gambling
- movies
- music.

Education

- There are many courses you can take online.
- All students routinely use the internet in order to do research.
- Immense stores of knowledge are available.

Financial transactions

- Most people bank online.
- New methods of payment are continually being developed.

Control

- Devices can be controlled remotely via internet links.
- Smart houses allow heating and lighting to be controlled.
- Burglar alarms can be set and responded to.

Commerce/advertising

- Internet shopping is replacing a lot of physical shopping.

Bandwidth

- The usefulness of the internet is affected by available **bandwidth**.
- Ever increasing bandwidths are needed to cope with the increasing demand for data. Movies, pictures and music are particularly demanding of bandwidth. More people are using streaming services such as the BBC iPlayer and Netflix to watch TV and movies.
- The availability of adequate bandwidth is patchy, with some countries and some parts of countries receiving a better service than others.

> **Bandwidth** In network terms, bandwidth refers to the number of bits of data that can be sent or received in a given time. It is normally measured in Mbit/s (megabits per second). Typical bandwidths are:
> - ADSL: 8 Mbit/s
> - ethernet: 10 Mbit/s
> - wireless 802.11g: 54 Mbit/s
> - fast ethernet: 100 Mbit/s.

> **Revision activity**
>
> Take a look at a map produced by Ofcom to see variations in bandwidth in the UK: http://maps.ofcom.org.uk/broadband/
>
> Find out the maximum bandwidth on your current internet and LAN connections. There are various speed-testing facilities available online

World wide web

REVISED

This is the collection of billions of web pages, stored on servers around the world. Often simply called 'the web'. The pages are potentially accessible anywhere, subject to copyright and government restrictions. They are all based on **HTML**.

Web pages are interpreted and displayed by browser software.

Web pages often incorporate:
- interactivity
- multimedia displays.

> **HTML (hypertext markup language)** A text-based language that uses **tags**. You can produce basic web pages using any plain-text editor. Web pages commonly have **links**.
>
> **Tags** Mark out elements on a web page to indicate to a browser how to display or process the element.
>
> **Links** Sensitive spots on a web page that connect to other pages or parts of the same page.

Now test yourself

TESTED

1 Distinguish between the internet and the world wide web.

Answer on page 156

Standards

The success of the internet depends to a great extent on the adoption of common standards. Standards ensure that resources can be accessed and used by a wide variety of computers, operating systems and applications.

Examples of common standards supporting and supported by the web are:

Standard	Meaning	Use
HTML	Hypertext mark-up language	Writing web pages for display.
XML	Extensible mark-up language	A text-based means of describing data. XML complements HTML by providing a way to store data for reuse. It separates data from HTML, thereby simplifying updates.
HTTP	Hypertext transfer protocol	Client–server protocol for requesting (client) and delivering (server) resources such as HTML files.
CSS	Cascading style sheets	Define how HTML elements are to be displayed. CSS files are stored separately from the HTML they affect.
Unicode		Character code designed to display over a million different characters.
Flash®		Multimedia platform for creating and displaying graphics. Less popular than in the past, often replaced by HTML5.
Silverlight®		A Microsoft® platform for producing multimedia and other web applications, similar to Flash. Like Flash, it is largely superseded by HTML5 and is not supported by all browsers.

Other file standards are commonly used on web pages such as:

Standard	Meaning	Use
PDF	Portable document format	To display documents exactly as intended
JPEG	Joint photographic experts group	A lossy compressed form of graphic storage
GIF	Graphics interchange format	A lossless compressed image file format
MPEG	Motion picture experts group	A compression standard for audio visual and data files

> **Revision activity**
>
> Make a few linked web pages, using a text editor. Use a CSS file to modify their appearance.

JavaScript®

This is a scripting language that runs in browsers. It is used to write scripts that control the behaviour of web page elements. It is a:
- high-level
- dynamically typed

interpreted language.

Together with HTML and CSS, JavaScript is one of the three essential web technologies. It can be run by any browser without the need for **plug-ins**.

JavaScript can be used for a wide variety of purposes such as:
- animating elements
- loading page content.
- validating web forms.

Java®

Java is not the same as JavaScript. Java is a compiled language. It is often used to write embedded applets to run in web pages. Java is compiled to an intermediate code called **bytecode**.

Bytecode runs in a **runtime environment**. This needs to be available on the computer in order to run Java applets. It provides a virtual machine which is an abstraction of a real computer and is useful in running applications on a variety of real platforms. It runs programs in an isolated **sandbox** which is intended to protect the computer from any damaging code.

> **Plug-in** Software that adds a feature to an application. Common examples include:
> - the ability to use a new video format
> - browser plug-ins such as Adobe® Flash® Player
> - the Java plug-in, which can run a Java applet.
>
> **Bytecode** A form of object code that is processed by a virtual machine; that is, by software, rather than by a hardware computer.
>
> **Java runtime environment** A collection of resources that allows the development and running of programs in the Java programming language.
>
> **Sandbox** A means of isolating untrusted programs, allowing them to run but not to access the host system or input devices.

Search engines

REVISED

Search engines are web-based software utilities that enable users to find resources on the web.

Search engines use software robots to collect and index words on web pages.

Meta tags are often added to web pages by web developers to help their pages be found. They can be harvested by web-crawling robots but are not part of the displayed page.

Pagerank algorithm™

A Level only

Google developed the Pagerank algorithm to make searches more useful.

The Pagerank algorithm:
- assigns a rank to a page based on the search term used and indications of relevance
- is forgiving with spelling mistakes
- attempts to deal with millions of pages in a useful way
- makes use of inward links to a site to assess its popularity and hence usefulness
- assigns inward links a rank as well
- regularly recalculates page ranks.

The Pagerank algorithm is given as:

$$PR(A) = (1 - d) + d\ (PR(T1)/C(T1) + ... + PR(Tn)/C(Tn))$$

where:
- PR(A) is the PageRank of page A
- PR(Ti) is the PageRank of pages Ti, which link to page A
- C(Ti) is the number of outbound links on page Ti
- d is a damping factor, which can be set between 0 and 1.

Client-side/server-side processing

REVISED

With any interaction between a user (client) and a server on the internet, data can be processed at either end.

Client-side processing is normally carried out by JavaScript scripts. Advantages of client-side processing are:
- web traffic is reduced
- the server does less processing
- there are fewer delays if data is processed locally
- data can be validated before being sent to the server.

Disadvantages of server-side processing are:
- databases have to be located on the server to be accessible to all users
- server-side databases must be protected from malicious or otherwise damaging interference.

Compression

REVISED

Data transmitted across the internet needs to be compressed where possible.

Compression reduces file sizes. This is to:
- reduce download times
- make best use of bandwidth
- reduce file storage requirements.

There are two different approaches to compression.

Lossy

Some data is stripped out to reduce file size.

The data removed is chosen to have the least importance.

Lossy is typically used in image and video files and music files, where it is less likely to be noticed by human observation.

Files compressed by lossy methods cannot be reinstated to their original detail.

Examples of lossy formats: JPEG, MPEG and MP3.

Lossless

Some files must not be degraded, for example a computer program will not work correctly if data is removed from it.

Lossless retains all the data by encoding it.

The original file can be regenerated.

Dictionary encoding

A Level only

The compression algorithm builds an index where each data item is recorded along with an index reference. The compressed file then consists of the dictionary plus the sequence of occurrences.

Example

Dictionary:

Reference	Data
1	if
2	you
3	are
4	not
5	fired
6	with
7	enthusiasm
8	will
9	be

A message can be constructed by supplying the dictionary and the words used; that is: 1234567289567.

Run-length encoding

This makes use of redundant data, so that if a data item occurs multiple times, the item is stored once in an index along with the number of repetitions. For example, part of an image with many adjacent blue pixels could be stored in an index by storing the start location and the number of repetitions.

Encryption

REVISED

Because of the public nature of the internet, it is important to protect data from unauthorised viewing or use. Encryption is commonly used.

Simple methods such as the Caesar cipher can be used, where letters are displaced by a known amount, for example a displacement of 4 would produce the following look-up table:

Plain text letter: ABCDEFGHIJKLMNOPQRSTUVWXYZ

Cipher letter: EFGHIJKLMNOPQRSTUVWXYZABCD

The number 4 is the key.

This is too simple for serious encryption so it is more common to use elaborate algorithms with much bigger keys, as described on page 167.

Hashing algorithms

These are described on page 96. They can be used to produce and check passwords.

- The password is transformed by the hashing algorithm.
- The transformed version is stored.
- It is impossible to regenerate the password from the hashed version.
- But applying the algorithm to the next login attempt will regenerate the hashed value which can be checked.

Exam practice

1 Distinguish between Java and JavaScript.   [4]
2 What is the role of a CSS file on a web page?   [4]
3 Distinguish between HTML and XML.   [5]
4 Describe how a file may be compressed with lossless compression techniques. [4]
5 Identify two situations where lossy compression is not acceptable.   [2]

Answers on page 168

Summary

- The internet is a network of networks. It is reliable, vendor independent and fast.
- It is an infrastructure. It is not the same as the world wide web, which is the collection of web pages.
- The internet has an enormous number of uses, which range from information exchange to entertainment and control of devices. These uses are being added to all the time.
- The internet is largely funded by advertising and other commercial interests.
- Usefulness of the internet is affected by available bandwidth. This is being increased all the time, although it is variable within and between countries.
- The appetite for bandwidth grows all the time, especially with more entertainment being supplied via the internet.
- The world wide web is the collection of web pages. These are written using HTML plus a variety of other supporting technologies. Particularly important are the addition of facilities provided by CSS and JavaScript.

- The internet's success is very much a consequence of the adoption of common standards.
- The world wide web is made usable by means of search engines. Search engines use innovative algorithms to return the most useful results for users.
- Internet sessions involve an interaction between client software (the user's browser or apps) and the server applications.
- The vast amount of data being sent over the internet has resulted in the need for compression algorithms to minimise traffic without impacting too much on usability.
- The public nature of the internet has required ever increasing levels of security and powerful encryption techniques.

Topic 4 Legal, ethical, moral and social issues

18 Computer law and ethical, moral and social issues

Computer law

REVISED

There are a number of acts of parliament that apply to the use of computer technology in the UK.

Computer Misuse Act (1990)

The Computer Misuse Act (1990) makes unauthorised access illegal.

Under the provisions of the act it is a criminal offence to:
- make unauthorised access to computer materials:
  - with intent to commit or facilitate further offences
  - with intent to impair, or with recklessness as to impair operation of computers, and so on.

The first provision essentially refers to unauthorised access (commonly called 'hacking').

The second provision refers to anything that impairs the performance of a computer system, including the distribution of viruses.

Features used to minimise these threats include:
- digital signatures or certificates that use encrypted messages to confirm the identity of the sender
- SSL (secure socket layer), a protocol that enables encrypted links between computers to ensure the security of a transaction
- user IDs, passwords and access rights, used for basic identification of users and their legitimate rights to access specific data
- anti-malware software, such as anti-virus and anti-spyware applications, used to identify and remove suspicious software on a computer system
- **Firewalls** – applications that sit between the system and external access to prevent certain types of data and users accessing the system, or simply to deny access to all external users
  - Firewalls are the principal defence against Denial of Service (DoS) attacks, where a user or group of users saturate the service with requests in order to make the service unavailable to other users.

> **Firewalls** Various combinations of hardware and software that can isolate a network from the outside world. They are configurable to allow or deny access to certain addresses or certain types of data.

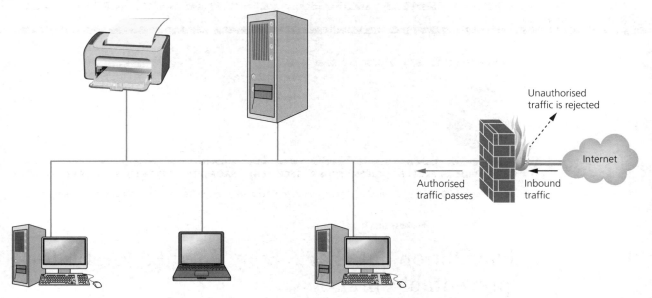

Figure 18.1 A firewall allows authorised traffic but denies access to unauthorised traffic from outside the system

Data Protection Act (1998)

The Data Protection Act (1998) sets out the requirements for the control of stored data about individuals.

There are eight provisions in the Data Protection Act (1998):
1 Data should be processed fairly and lawfully (that is, the data must not be obtained by deception and the purpose of the data being collected should be revealed to the **data subject**).
2 Data should only be used for the purpose specified to the Data Protection Agency and should not be disclosed to other parties without the necessary permission.
3 Data should be relevant and not excessive.
4 Data should be accurate and up to date.
5 Data should only be kept for as long as is necessary.
6 Individuals have the right to access data kept about them and should be able to check and update the data if necessary.
7 Security must be in place to prevent unauthorised access to the data.
8 Data may not be transferred outside the EU unless the country has adequate data-protection legislation.

> **Data subject** The individual about whom the data is stored.

The **data controller** in an organisation is responsible for the accuracy and security of data kept about the data subject.

There are some exemptions to the Data Protection Act (1998) principles:
● National security – any data processed in relation to national security is exempt from the Act.
● Crime and taxation – any data used to detect or prevent crime or to assist with the collection of taxes is exempt from the Act.
● Domestic purposes – any data used solely for individual, family or household use is exempt from the Act.

> **Data controller** The person who is responsible for implementing the provisions of the DPA within an organisation.

www.independent.co.uk/news/business/news/playstation-data-hack-sony-fined-250000-for-preventable-breach-8464651.html

THE INDEPENDENT TUESDAY 24 FEBRUARY 2015

| NEWS | VIDEO | PEOPLE | VOICES | SPORT | TECH | LIFE | PROPERTY | ARTS + ENTS | OSCARS | TRAVEL |

UK / World / Business / People / Science / Environment / Media / Technology / Education / Images / Ob

News > Business > Business News

PlayStation data hack: Sony fined £250,000 for 'preventable' breach

JAMIE GRIERSON   Thursday 24 January 2013

f SHARE   **y** TWEET   **g+** SHARE   **@** REDDIT   **in** SHARE   **<**   Shares: 25   PRINT A A A

Gaming giant Sony has been fined £250,000 by the data watchdog for a breach that compromised the personal information of millions of PlayStation users.

The Information Commissioner's Office (ICO) issued the penalty after it found the attack on the Sony PlayStation Network in April 2011 could have been prevented.

Personal information including customers' payment card details, names, addresses, email addresses, dates of birth and account passwords were exposed.

David Smith, ICO deputy commissioner and director of data protection, said: "If you are responsible for so many payment card details and log-in details, then keeping that personal data secure has to be your priority.

In this case that just didn't happen, and when the database was targeted - albeit in a determined criminal attack - the security

www.independent.co.uk/news/media/   'es in place were simply not good enough.

Figure 18.2 Organisations can be prosecuted under the DPA for breaches of data security

Copyright Designs and Patents Act (CDPA) (1988)

The Copyright Designs and Patents Act (CDPA) (1988) protects the intellectual property rights of individuals and organisations.

Under the Act, it is illegal to copy, modify or distribute software or other intellectual property without the relevant permission.

This Act also covers video and audio where peer-to-peer streaming has had a significant impact on the income of the copyright owners.

Regulation of Investigatory Powers Act (RIPA) (2000)

The Regulation of Investigatory Powers Act (RIPA) (2000) gives certain bodies the right to monitor communications and internet activity.

The Regulation of Investigatory Powers Act provides certain public bodies, such as the police and other government departments, with the right to:
- demand ISPs provide access to a customer's communications
- allow mass surveillance of communications
- demand ISPs fit equipment to facilitate surveillance
- demand access be granted to protected information
- allow monitoring of an individual's internet activities
- prevent the existence of such interception activities being revealed in court.

The Act is intended to allow suitable authorities access to communications to prevent criminal or terrorist activities.

There was some concern about the range of public bodies with powers under this Act when it was first introduced.

There are examples of this Act being used for reasons other than monitoring criminal or terrorist activities.

Figure 18.3 Media reports of RIPA being used against journalists

Communications Act (2003)

The Act is in place to deal with communications that contain credible threats of violence, such as trolling or stalking, or communications that contain material grossly offensive to identified individuals and intended to cause harm.

The Communications Act (2003) has several provisions that impact on the use of computer technology.

Among the provisions in the Act are that it is illegal to:

- access an internet connection with no intention to pay for the service, making it a crime to piggyback onto other people's WiFi without their permission
- send offensive communications using any communications system, including social media.

Those who repeat the messages are also subject to the provisions of this Act, and re-tweeting an offensive message may be illegal.

Equality Act (2010)

The Equality Act (2010) identifies certain protected characteristics and makes it illegal to discriminate against anyone with those characteristics, either by direct discrimination, or by indirect discrimination.

This Act has implications for those who provide web-based services.

Section 29(1) of the 2010 Act says that:

A person concerned with the provision of a service to the public or a section of the public (for payment or not) must not discriminate against a person requiring the service by not providing the person with the service.

There are various features available to make websites more accessible:

- Screen readers for the blind user are applications that sift through the HTML to identify the content and read this out to the user.
- For those with partial or poor sight, options for larger text or a screen magnifier may be appropriate.
- The choice of font is also an important issue; sites using very blocky or cursive fonts may be very difficult to read for those with visual disabilities.
- Tagging images with an audio description for those who are partially sighted or blind provides some access to the graphical content of a website.
- Choosing contrasting colours for text and background will also make the text stand out more effectively for those who are partially sighted or colour blind; avoiding those colour combinations that are most difficult for colour-blind people will improve accessibility.
- While deaf users have the ability to access websites in much the same way as those with normal hearing, any soundtracks should be provided as subtitles or as a transcript.

> **Revision activity**
>
> Research software and hardware features that help those with disabilities make use of computer technology and systems and how computer systems and hardware can assist those with disabilities.

> **Exam tip**
>
> These topics are likely to be asked under broad headings as level of response questions. Research news stories surrounding each of the Acts and use these to illustrate your responses. Remember there are two sides to each argument so try to present a balanced argument looking at both sides of any issue and reach a conclusion based on the evidence you provide.

Moral and ethical issues

REVISED

Computers in the workplace

Computer technology in various forms plays a major part in the workplace:

- Computer technology has changed the skillset required from the modern workforce.
- The way we access services has changed the job market significantly with fewer traditional high street and office roles.
- The workforce is subject to monitoring by computer technology to assess their productivity, the way they work and their effectiveness.

Automated decision-making

Given the speed with which many decisions must be made, many automated decisions can only be made by computer technology.

- Computers are able to analyse millions of data items quickly and accurately.
- They use algorithms to process the data and reach decisions.

> **Revision activity**
>
> Research how roles in the workplace have been affected by the introduction of computer technology, roles that have been created by the widespread use of computer technology and how the use of computer technology has impacted upon roles in the workplace. You can use this research to provide evidence to use in your responses to level of response questions.

- The quality of the decision will depend upon:
  - the accuracy and completeness of the data
  - the predictability of the situation
  - the quality of the algorithm.

Examples of automated decision-making include:
- electrical power distribution requires rapid responses to changing circumstances to avoid disastrous consequences
- in an emergency response to a major incident, automated decision making can help to deploy resources quickly and effectively
- plant automation, for example chemical plants or distribution centres, improves efficiency and health and safety
- airborne collision avoidance systems are essential for safety
- credit assessment in banks
- trading in shares and commodities.

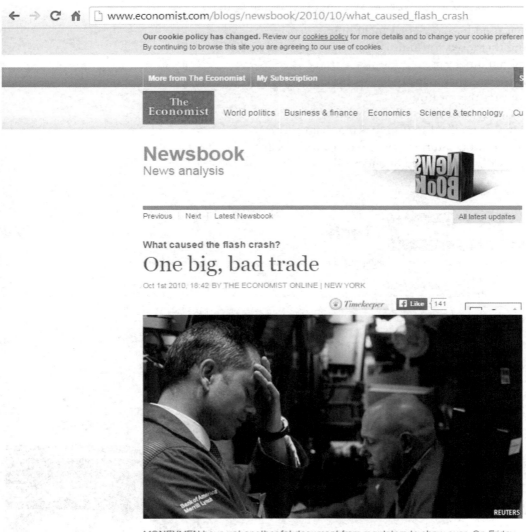

Figure 18.4 The 2010 flash crash

Artificial intelligence

Artificial intelligence programs are designed to learn from experience and much of the development in this area is based on neural networks, which attempt to emulate the way the human brain works.

Tasks that are simple for humans can be quite complex for computers, for example recognising objects and people, or deciding if a station platform is full or not.

Many artificial intelligence systems are based on expert systems. Expert systems have three components:
- a knowledge base including the collected expert knowledge often as 'if.. then' rules
- an inference engine that searches the knowledge base to identify potential responses
- an interface to communicate with the user or system it is working with.

Artificial intelligence is used in many areas including:
- credit-card checking that looks for unusual patterns in credit-card use to identify potential fraudulent use
- speech recognition systems that identify keywords and patterns in the spoken word to interpret the meaning
- medical diagnosis systems used to self-diagnose illness from the symptoms and to support medical staff in making diagnoses
- control systems that monitor, interpret and predict events to provide real-time process control, for example in chemical plants.

Figure 18.5 An AI system is used to manage the repairs to the Hong Kong subway system

Environmental issues

REVISED

Computers are made from some toxic materials that need to be recycled carefully if they are not to cause significant pollution. Some of these toxic elements are:

- airborne dioxins
- polychlorinated biphenyls (PCBs)
- cadmium
- chromium
- radioactive isotopes
- mercury.

To avoid the cost of recycling and recovering these dangerous elements many computers are simply shipped off for disposal to countries with lower environmental standards. In many cases the waste is picked over by people to recover the valuable metals, exposing them to significant dangers.

Modern computer systems consume large amounts of power and data centres use significant amounts of electricity. Estimates for 2014 suggest that data centres used more energy than the aviation industry.

Figure 18.6 Picking over discarded computer equipment to extract metals

Censorship and the internet

REVISED

Internet censorship is the deliberate suppression of what can be accessed or published on the internet.

- Governments or organisations may impose these restrictions for various reasons: to limit access to socially unacceptable material or to limit access to what they regard as dangerous information.
- The extent to which the internet is censored varies from country to country, depending on the political and social situations in those countries.
- Censorship is usually carried out centrally or by internet service providers at the request of or under instruction from governments.
- Total control of information through censorship is very difficult to apply unless there is a single central censor.
- Despite censorship many people will still share information through underlying data transfer networks including file-sharing networks, for example the deep web that cannot be found by traditional search engines.

- Access to websites is filtered by reference to blacklists that are set up with unacceptable sites and through dynamic examination of the website for unacceptable content.
- The main categories being blocked by ISPs in the UK include extremist politics, extreme pornography and sites that infringe copyright.

Monitoring behaviour

REVISED

People are increasingly being monitored by computer technology, for example:
- performance in a workplace role
- known criminals with tagging devices
- how drivers drive, with in-vehicle devices, to reduce insurance costs
- social media posts and activities by the press and employers
- internet activity while at work by employers.

Once data is on the internet it is difficult to remove and may be available for many years after the event and may be accessed by employers, potential employers, the authorities or the press in the future.

Figure 18.7 Fifteen miners were fired after posting a video on social media showing a breach of behaviour policy at work

Analysing personal information

Data about individuals is collected by many organisations and while the data collected may be harmless in isolation, when combined with data collected elsewhere it could create issues for the individual.

The DPA provides suitable legislation about sharing data between organisations but the problem will often not be identified until data is shared in contravention of the Act.

Data is a valuable commodity and is used to analyse shopping and leisure activities to focus advertising more effectively.

Data mining is an automated process that searches for patterns in large data sets to predict events.

- Data mining is a valuable tool in the fight against organised crime; data about individual activities including social media, financial transactions, travel, internet histories and shared contact details have provided valuable information in the fight against crime and terrorism.
- In business it is used to identify patterns to inform strategic business decisions. The data can be used to predict future sales and hence stock requirements and effective and targeted marketing strategies to improve business profitability.
- In science and engineering, analysis of human DNA sequences and matching this to medical information has led to the development of effective treatments for various conditions.

> **Exam tip**
>
> Identify examples for each of these areas that can be used to illustrate your arguments if there is a question on these topic areas in your exam.

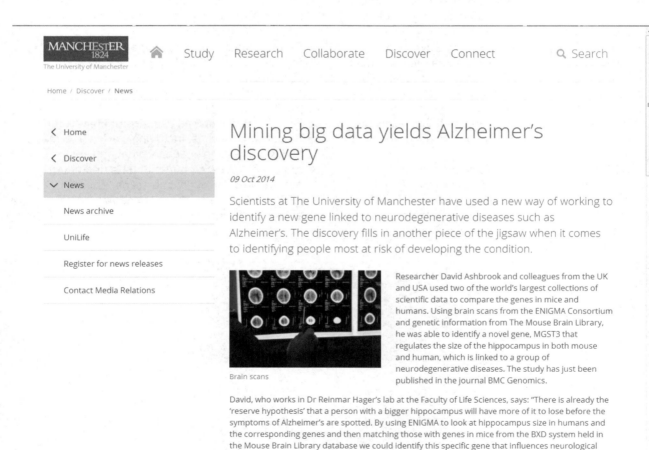

Figure 18.8 Research taking place at Manchester University shows how data mining can lead to new discoveries

18 Computer law and ethical, moral and social issues

Exam practice

1 What are the implications under the DPA for a mail order company who keep detailed records of customers and wish to share these with a sister company selling a different range of products? [4]
2 What are the potential consequences of posting images and thoughts on social media? [4]
3 What measures should a website developer put into place to ensure they do not disadvantage disabled users? [6]
4 Computers are used to monitor workplace communications and progress. Is this acceptable or is it an infringement of civil liberties? [6]
5 How are computers used to monitor everyday activities and in what ways does this benefit us as individuals? [6]

Answers on page 168

Summary

- The Computer Misuse Act (1990) makes unauthorised access illegal; this is the act that makes hacking and the distribution of viruses and other malware a criminal offence.
- The Data Protection Act (1998) sets out the rights of individuals and the responsibilities of organisations regarding storage of personal data.
- The Copyrights, Designs and Patents Act (1988) protects the intellectual property rights of individuals and organisations.
- The Regulation of Investigatory Powers Act (2000) gives certain public bodies the right to monitor communications and internet activity.
- The Communications Act (2003) is in place to deal with communications that contain threats of violence, such as trolling or stalking, or offensive material intended to harm the individual.
- Web-based services have responsibilities under the Equality Act (2010) to ensure that they do not discriminate against individuals who have any disability. They need to ensure measures are in place to make their services available to all users.

- Automated decision-making is used where the amount of data or the response speed make it impossible for a human to react effectively.
- Artificial intelligence programs learn from experience. They are often based on the expert system model with a knowledge base, inference engine and a user interface.
- Computers are made from toxic chemicals, and disposal of redundant equipment needs to be carefully managed to avoid pollution and harm to individuals.
- Censorship of the internet varies from country to country, but is used to prevent access to materials the governments regard as dangerous, criminal, offensive or in breach of the local legislation.
- People are monitored using computer systems for various reasons, including work performance and criminal, social and internet activity.
- Analysing large amounts of data, including personal data, reveals patterns. These patterns can be of shopping habits, social activity, criminal activity, information to inform business strategies or the development of new medical treatments.

Now test yourself answers

Topic 2

Chapter 4

1 The value of 1 is printed again and again until stack overflow occurs.

2 Insert a condition to terminate the endless loop, such as in this example:

```
def recurse(number):
    print(number)
    number+=1
    if (number<100):  ←——— terminating
        recurse(number)        condition
    return;

recurse(1)
```

Chapter 5

1 The list holding the data must be sorted.

2 (a) 1000

(b) 10

3 Starting at the beginning of the list, each item is compared to the one next to it. If they are out of order they are swapped. When the algorithm gets to the end of the list it goes back to the start. Once it has gone all the way through the list without making any swaps the list is in order.

4 The pivot is used to divide the list into sub-lists (those bigger and smaller than it). The pivots at any stage are the sorted items in the list.

5 A* search uses heuristics to take into account whether a given path moves closer to or further away from the destination node. Both algorithms will find the shortest path, but A* search in many cases will find it more quickly.

Topic 3

Chapter 6

1 JavaScript is a high-level language. It is machine independent and uses English and mathematical notation rather than processor instructions.

2 BRA, BRP and BRZ all branch to the location they name.

BRA always branches; BRP only branches if the value in the accumulator is positive (including 0); BRZ only branches if the value in the accumulator is 0.

3 LDA loads the value at the specified location into the accumulator.

4 A program to triple a number:

```
        INP
        STA num
        ADD num
        ADD num
        OUT
        HLT
num DAT
```

5 A program to subtract 1 from a number:

```
        INP
        SUB one
        OUT
        HLT
one DAT 1
```

6 A high-level equivalent in Python:

```
number = input("Enter a number")
if number < 10:
    print(0)
else:
    print(10)
```

7 A program that triples numbers under 100 and doubles other numbers:

```
        INP
        STA num
        SUB hundred
        BRP triple
        LDA num
        ADD num
        ADD num
        OUT
        HLT
Triple   LDA num
        ADD num
        OUT
        HLT
Hundred DAT 100
Num     DAT
```

8 A program to keep asking for a number until a number greater than 10 is entered:

```
start INP
        STA num
        LDA ten
        SUB num
        BRP start
        HLT
ten     DAT 10
num     DAT
```

9 A program that asks for a number then prints that many 1s:

```
        INP
        BRZ end
        SUB one
        STA count
start   SUB one
        STA count
        LDA one
        OUT
        LDA count
        BRP start
end     HLT
one     DAT 1
count   DAT
```

10

Addressing mode	Value in accumulator after LDA 4
Direct	6
Indirect	9
Immediate	4
Indexed (8 in the index register)	32

11 A class is a template that describes the attributes and methods that objects of its type will have. An object is an instance of a class.

12
```
class Mansion inherits House
  private fountain

  public procedure new(givenDoor
  Colour, givenGarden, givenFloors,
  givenFountain)
      fountain=givenFountain
super.new(givenDoorColour, givenFloors,
givenGarden)
  endprocedure

  public procedure changeFloors
  (givenFloors)
      if Floors>= 2 then
        floors=givenFloors
      endif
  endprocedure

endclass
```

Chapter 7

1 A compression program is a utility. It is a small program with one purpose that helps with system upkeep.

2 A desktop publishing package is an application. It allows users to make posters, leaflets, flyers, and so on.

3 An operating system:
   - manages the hardware of the system
   - manages programs installed and being run
   - manages the security of the system
   - provides an interface between the user and the computer.

4 A student might use a multi-tasking operating system simultaneously to run a:
   - web browser to research on the internet
   - word processor to write an essay
   - media player to play music
   - virus checker to keep the system free of viruses.

5 Virtual memory is used to store pages not immediately needed when physical memory is full.

6 Paging is the splitting of memory according to equally sized physical divisions. Segmentation is the splitting of memory according to the logical divisions of its contents.

7 In First Come First Served, jobs are queued as they come in. Once one is completed the next one is processed. This may mean some never get processed.

8 The priority of an interrupt determines when it gets serviced. An interrupt can only disturb a process of a lower priority than itself.

9 A device driver is a program that allows the operating system to control hardware devices, such as printers.

10 Advantage: Intermediate code is architecture independent, able to run off any device with a supporting virtual machine.

   Disadvantage: The end program runs more slowly than it would with native code due to the extra layer of processing needed to run the virtual machine.

Chapter 8

1 A programmer may use an interpreter during development. This means that when testing their code, they don't have to repeatedly wait for compilation. Interpreters also tend to flag up errors as they are encountered whilst the program executes. This can help with the debugging process.

2 A high-level language uses a mixture of English and mathematical notation and is much easier for humans to read than low-level languages, which use instructions for the processor. High-level languages are processor independent.

3 • Lexical analysis
   - Syntax analysis
   - Code generation
   - Code optimisation

4 The symbol table stores the variable and subroutine names, data types and scope.

5 Libraries save programmers the time they would spend writing code, which has already been produced by others. They allow programmers to use code that may require particular areas of expertise to produce, such as cryptography or graphics. Programmers have the confidence this code is already tested.

6 A linker combines the pieces of code for a program, including from libraries, into a single executable piece of code.

Chapter 9

1 A feasibility study checks whether a project is:
   - technically possible
   - deliverable within the given timeframe
   - possible within the given budget
   - ethical and legal
   - feasible with the company's current workforce.

2 Alpha testing is the testing of software's functionality by people within the company producing it.

3 User documentation explains how a system is used. It may contain descriptions of installation, how to carry out tasks on the system, troubleshooting and frequently asked questions.

4 The prototype is used for evaluation by the user at the end of each iteration. This evaluation is used to feed into the next iteration. By the end of the process, the prototype has become the final product.

5
   - Determine requirements
   - Analysis
   - Design
   - Coding
   - Testing
   - Maintenance

6 The spiral model is a risk-focused software lifecycle. It is iterative; each iteration involves determining objectives; identifying and resolving risks; developing and testing; and planning the next iteration.

Chapter 10

1
   - Keyboard
   - Mouse
   - Joystick
   - Scanner
   - Microphone
   - Touchscreen
   - Trackpad
   - Webcam
   - Barcode scanner
   - Fingerprint scanner

2
   - Monitor
   - Projector
   - Speaker
   - Motor
   - LED
   - Printer
   - Plotter
   - 3D printer
   - Headphones
   - Laser cutter

3 Most schools will use a combination of tape drives, RAID and offsite storage.

4 The control unit orchestrates the movement of data around the CPU and memory during the fetch–decode–execute cycle. During this process it decodes instructions.

5 Any example with LDA, ADD, SUB or INP will change the contents of the accumulator.

6 One from:
   RAM is volatile; ROM is non-volatile.
   RAM can be written to; ROM can't.

7 Multiple instructions multiple data is parallel processing where different instructions are applied to different pieces of data simultaneously.

8 Single instruction multiple data is parallel processing where the same instruction is applied to different pieces of data simultaneously.

9 CISC has more addressing modes than RISC.

Chapter 11

1 (a) 130
  (b) 193
  (c) 216
2 (a) 10001100
  (b) (0)1000100
  (c) 11001000
3 (a) 00111000
  (b) 10111000
  (c) 11111101
4 (a) 40
  (b) −68
  (c) −49
5 (a) 1A
  (b) 5C
  (c) AF
6 (a) 101010111100
  (b) 101001011101
  (c) 1011101111000011
7 (a) 165
  (b) 95
  (c) 734

Chapter 12

1 (a) 11110
  (b) 11001
  (c) 10110
  (d) 1011
  (e) 101
2 (a) 11001110 (−79 + 29 = −50)
  (b) 11110010 (−113 + 99 = −14)
3 (a) 35 −   00100011
     1's comp   11011100
     add 1   11011101
     67 −   01000011
     Add   (1) 00100000
  (b) 66 −   01000010
     1's comp   10111101
     Add 1   10111110
     108   01101100
     Add   (1) 00101010
  (c) 65 −   01000001
     1's comp   10111110
     Add 1   10111111
     53   00110101
     Add   11110100
4 (a) 1.25
  (b) −2.5
  (c) 0.375
5 (a) 5.5
  (b) −0.3125
6 (a) 0110100000 000001
  (b) 1011000000 000010
  (c) 0110000000 111110
7 (a) 01101(1) 011
  (b) 01110(1) 001
     Note how the last digit in the mantissa is lost; this is overflow.
  (c) 01111 001
  (d) 01000 110
8

0	0	1	1	0	1	1	0	Operand
1	0	1	0	1	0	1	0	MASK
0	0	1	0	0	0	1	0	AND
1	0	1	1	1	1	1	0	OR
1	0	0	1	1	1	0	0	XOR

9 Mask with 100010001 using XOR.
10 Mask with 010001001 using AND.

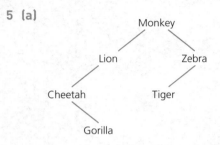

Chapter 13

1

Initial pointers							
		9					
Top	12	12	12		17		
	7	7	7	7	7	7	
Bottom	3	3	3	3	3	3	3

2

Initial pointers						
Start	5	5				
	3	3	3			
End	7	7	7	7	7	
		12	12	12	12	12
				9	9	9
						6

3 (a) Jane

(b) (i) and **(ii)**

Names()	0	1	2	3	4	5
0	Alan	Kuldeep	Li	Sarah	Harry	Mary
1	Jane	Navdeep	Charles	Joe	Jane	Irina
2	Wendy	Deborah	Dillip	Umar	Johan	Hua

(c) Navdeep

Charles

Joe

4 (a)

Start pointer 3		
1	Monkey	4
2	Lion	1
3	Cheetah	5
4	Zebra	0
5	Gorilla	2
6		

(b)

Start pointer 3		
1	Monkey	4
2	Lion	
3	Cheetah	5
4	Zebra	0
5	Gorilla	1
6		

(c)

Start pointer 3		
1	Monkey	6
2	Lion	
3	Cheetah	5
4	Zebra	0
5	Gorilla	1
6	Tiger	4

5 (a)

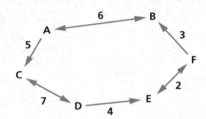

(b) Monkey, Lion, Cheetah, Gorilla, Zebra, Tiger

(c) Gorilla, Cheetah, Lion, Tiger, Zebra, Monkey

6

7 (a)

STACK				D		E			
			C	C	C	C	C		
		B	B	B	B	B	B	B	
	A	A	A	A	A	A	A	A	A
VISITED	A	B	C	D		E			

(b)

QUEUE		B		C	C	C		D		
					E					
VISITED	A	B		C	E			D		
CURRENT	A	A	B	B	B	B	C	C	D	

8 (a) 213

(b) 99

Chapter 14

1 (a)

A	B	C	(A∧B)	¬C	(A∧B)∨¬C
0	0	0	0	1	1
0	0	1	0	0	0
0	1	0	0	1	1
0	1	1	0	0	0
1	0	0	0	1	1
1	0	1	0	0	0
1	1	0	1	1	1
1	1	1	1	0	1

(b)

A	B	C	(A∧B)	¬(A∧B)	¬(A∧B)∨C
0	0	0	0	1	1
0	0	1	0	1	1
0	1	0	0	1	1
0	1	1	0	1	1
1	0	0	0	1	1
1	0	1	0	1	1
1	1	0	1	0	0
1	1	1	1	0	1

2 (a)

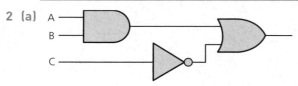

(b)

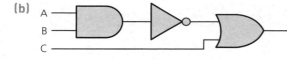

3 (a) ¬(A ∨ C) ∨ ¬(C ∨ D), which is the same as (¬A ∧ ¬C) ∨ (¬C ∧ ¬D)

(b) (B ∧ D) ∨ (¬B ∧ C)

4

CD\AB	00	01	11	10
00	0	1	1	1
01	0	1	1	1
11	0	1	1	0
10	0	1	1	0

B ∨ (A ∧ ¬C)

5 (a) A ∧ (B ∨ C) Distributive law

(b) =A ∧ (B ∨ C), which is the same as (A ∧ B) ∨ (A ∧ C)

(c) ¬ A ∨ (A ∧ B)

=(¬ A ∨ A) ∧ (¬ A ∨ B)

=1 ∧ (¬ A ∨ B)

= ¬ A ∨ B

so the expression simplifies to ¬ A ∨ B ∨ C

Chapter 15

1 Examples include:
- Emissions monitoring – needs to access diagnostic databases when trouble detected; made use of engine characteristic databases when manufactured
- Satnav – needs to access database of road maps and locations of interest
- ECU checking engine performance – accesses performance tables

2 Sales in a shop – it makes sense to store them in chronological order.

3 An address book – it is easier to find entries if the names are in alphabetical order.

4 Your other details such as name, date of birth and postcode will be indexed for quick searches to be made on those fields.

5 A structured persistent store of data on a computer system.

6 • Records
- Fields
- Tables

7 Data arranged in a logical and consistent pattern.

8 A simple one-table data store.

9 An address book.

10 With fixed-length fields, all the records are the same size however much data is stored in them. Variable length fields only use up the minimum amount of space required by the data.

11 Fixed-length fields are easier to write processing software for. A particular record can be found by fast forwarding to the appropriate place. Also, files made from fixed length fields can be planned to be of a predictable size.

12 No order.

13 The field(s) used to make each row of a table unique.

14 • To identify a row unambiguously.
- To link to the foreign keys of other tables.

15 (a) policy number. The policy number can uniquely identify a particular policy. All the other fields can be duplicated in other records.

16 The two fields `Student_number` and `Subject_number` taken together create a unique identity to each row.

17 Create a new field such as `Student_subject` or `Entry`, which can be made unique for each row.

18 Table Stock

stock_number, stock_name, number_in_ stock, supplier ref

Table Order

order_number, order_date, order_ quantity, stock_number

Table Supplier

supplier_ref, supplier_name, supplier_email

Chapter 16

1 • LAN: one limited area; WAN: covers large area.

• LAN: owned in total by the operating organisation; WAN: communication links owned by communication company.

• LAN: maintained by company's own technicians; WAN: parts may be maintained by other employees.

2 An abstraction of a network based on seven layers. It is non-proprietary and forms the basis of some other layered models.

3 It allows each layer to be designed and maintained independently. There is no need to address all layers when designing a network.

4 The link layer obtains data from the internet layer and places it as signals on the physical connections. It also receives signals from the physical layers and passes them as data to the internet layer.

5 A group of eight bits commonly used to designate an IP address.

6

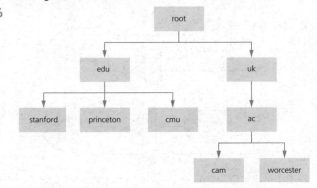

7 Examples include:

Some require:

• the entry of a captcha to prevent automated log-ins

• double password entry

• a graphic such as a QR code

• smart-card access

• biometric access

• memorable data (e.g. banks).

Chapter 17

1 The internet is a network of networks; it is an infrastructure. The world wide web is the collection of web pages that can be accessed through the internet.

Exam practice answers

Topic 1

Chapter 1

1 Situations that rely primarily on measurement and calculation, such as:
   - estimating the cost of a decorating job
   - predicting the time it will take to drive from A to B
   - forecasting weather over a limited time frame.

   (2 marks for each activity identified and described)

2 Examples should include situations where there is some unpredictability or a human factor as well as a data-based or calculated component, such as:
   - forecasting the result of a horse race
   - planning the layout of a shop
   - designing a new car.

   (2 marks each activity identified and described)

3 The top-down approach allows a large project to be separated into smaller modules (1 mark), which enables the task to be handed to more than one developer, thereby resulting in economies of time and expense. (1 mark)

4 (a) A way of managing complexity by representing (1 mark) functionality at different levels without recourse to the concrete world. (1 mark) Abstraction works by hiding much of the detail of a situation so that we can ignore the parts that we do not need (1 mark) when solving a part of the problem.

   (b) Any two correct examples, such as payroll system and booking system.

   In each case, produce a menu (1 mark), design the output. (1 mark)

   (Many other examples could be acceptable.)

Chapter 2

Answers are examples only, not definitive.

1 Display a map (1 mark) showing thickness of roads proportional to traffic flow. (1 mark) Take data from morning rush hour.

2 Think back to where you have been (1 mark) in reverse order. (1 mark) Visit each location and search.

3 (a) Some aspects are quantifiable and therefore computable (1 mark); others are a matter of feelings, interests or emotion and are not computable. (1 mark)

   (b) Examples include salary, living expenses, the number of openings currently available (2 marks for any two)

4 Example questions:
   - What are his anticipated earnings after graduation? (1 mark)
   - What are his living expenses during education? (1 mark)
   - What are the trends of similar shares over a ten-year period? (1 mark)

5
   - Think of activities that can take place simultaneously, such as cooking and serving. (1 mark)
   - Think about how customers can access different services simultaneously, such as getting a main course, a side salad and drinks. (1 mark)
   - Think about arranging the physical layout to allow simultaneous activities. (1 mark)

6 Arrange for inputs to occur from the cache (1 mark) at the same time as processing (1 mark); prefetch data that is likely to be needed (1 mark) to reduce data-access time.

7 (a)

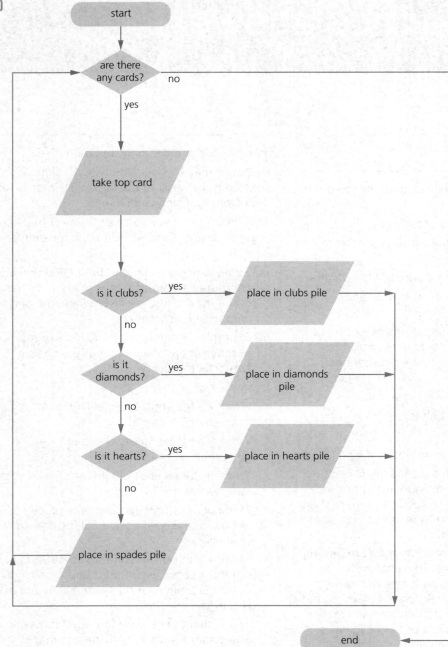

(b) Various possibilities, such as taking turns with the other person to pick up a card (1 mark) then apply the algorithm. (1 mark)

(c) Calculate the number of operations/decisions (1 mark) in each case. There is no need to take the speed of action into account. (1 mark)

Topic 2

Chapter 3

1 Some cases may be debatable.
   (a) A
   (b) A
   (c) B
   (d) C
   (e) C
   (1 mark for each correct answer)

2 Answers are examples only, not definitive.
   (a) • What is the mark-up of sales price over expenses?
      • Estimate expected sales.
      • Estimate costs of delay.
      • Collect and analyse market-research data.
      (1 mark for each sub-problem identified)
   (b) • Largely calculable.
      • All the data is obtainable. It can be estimated by using past statistics and research. It is unlikely to be totally accurate.
      • This can be calculated to an extent. Some intelligent guesswork will be needed as there will be unknowns.
      • This is mostly calculable, using statistics and projections, but experience plays a part too because human behaviour will be a factor.
      (2 marks for each well-argued point)

Chapter 4

1 The expression evaluates to true or false. (1 mark) Program control is passed to a different point (1 mark), the diversion is executed (1 mark) or not (1 mark), according to the Boolean expression.

2 A while loop is tested on entry (1 mark) and may not always be executed. A for loop is executed a fixed number of times, which is known in advance. (1 mark)

3 Global variables can be changed unexpectedly (1 mark) and may have effects in multiple parts of the program. (1 mark)

4 A value/data item passed to a function. (1 mark)

5 Reference: the address of the data item is passed. (1 mark) Any changes made by the function are retained. (1 mark) Value: a copy of the data item is passed. (1 mark) Changes made do not affect the original data. (1 mark)

6 A class is a blueprint for an object. (1 mark) The object is an instance of a class. (1 mark)

Chapter 5

1

A	B	C	D	E	F	G	H	I	J	K
0	1	2	3	4	5	6	7	8	9	10

LB   MP   UB

(0+10)/2 = 5 so the midpoint is 5

Location 5 is F, which is greater than E, so becomes the new upper bound.

A	B	C	D	E	F	G	H	I	J	K
0	1	2	3	4	5	6	7	8	9	10

LB   MP   UB

(0+5)/2 = 2.5

We will assume we round up so the midpoint is 3. (1 mark)

D is lower than E so the MP becomes the new LB.

A	B	C	D	E	F	G	H	I	J	K
0	1	2	3	4	5	6	7	8	9	10

        LB MP UB

(3+4)/2 = 3.5 which rounds up to 4.
Location 4 contains E. (1 mark)

A	B	C	D	E	F	G	H	I	J	K
0	1	2	3	4	5	6	7	8	9	10

        LB MP UB

2 Split into 1-item-large lists. (1 mark)

D		A		B		F		E		C

Merge each pair of lists. (1 mark)

A	D		B	F		E	C

Merge the sub lists again. As there an odd number, one will not get merged.

A	B	D	F		E	C

Merge the final two lists. (1 mark)

A	B	C	D	E	F

3 Pick an item as the pivot (can be any item – we will use C first). Create two sub-lists of those items higher and lower than the pivot.

Do the same with the sub-lists. (1 mark)

And again. (1 mark)

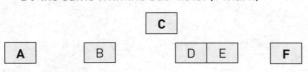

Until all items are pivots.

At which point they can be combined into a sorted list. (1 mark)

A	B	C	D	E	F

4 (a) n^3 (1 mark)

(b) Polynomial (1 mark)

5
- B starts as current node. Update A, D and F.
- D becomes current node. Update F but not I (as existing route is quicker).
- F becomes current node. Update C and H.
- A becomes current node. Update C but not B.
- H becomes the current node. Update E.
- C becomes the current node. A and F aren't updated as they have been visited and E isn't updated as it already has a lower value.
- I becomes the current node. J is the only connected unvisited node and is updated.
- E becomes the current node. G is updated to 125.
- J becomes the current node. G is not updated as 200 > 125.
- G is the current node so the algorithm stops.

Recorded on a table it should look as below:

Node	Shortest distance from B	Via
A	∞ 50	B
B	0	
C	∞ 85 75	F A
D	∞ 25	B
E	∞ 95	H
F	∞ 35	D
G	∞ 125	E
H	∞ 60	F
I	∞ 80	B
J	∞ 120	I

This gives the shortest route as 120 going from BD>FH>EG

(1 mark for rows B, D and F being correct, 1 mark for the remaining rows being correct, 1 mark for the correct route)

Topic 3

Chapter 6

1 High-level languages are easier to code with than low-level languages. (1 mark) They are closer to English and the same outcome can be achieved in fewer lines of code. (1 mark)

High-level languages are architecture-independent. (1 mark)

(1 mark for each point up to a maximum of 2)

2 Program to count from 1 to 100:

```
loop LDA count
OUT
ADD one
STA count
LDA hundred
SUB count
BRP loop
HLT
one DAT 1
hundred DAT 100
count DAT 1
```

(1 mark for printing number 1, 1 mark for the program counting up, 1 mark for it stopping at 100)

3 (a) With direct addressing, memory location can be accessed in fewer steps than with indirect addressing. (1 mark)

(b) Indirect addressing allows a wider range of values to be accessed (as no bits are used by the opcode) than direct addressing. (1 mark)

4 Inheritance could be used for the stock.

Books, magazines and DVDs could all inherit from stock. (1 mark)

FictionBook, NonFictionBook and ChildrensBook could all inherit from Book.

Inheritance could also be used for the staff. (1 mark)

Manager and Librarian could both inherit from StaffMember. (1 mark)

(1 mark for each point up to a maximum of 2)

5 Encapsulation is considered best practice as it prevents inconsistencies in data. It prevents attributes in an object from being changed in a way that could have unforeseen consequences. (1 mark)

6
```
class dog
    private colour
    public procedure new(givenColour)
        changeColour(givenColour)
    endprocedure
    public changeColour(givenColour)
        if givenColour=="black" or
        givenColour=="brown" or
        givenColour=="white" or
        givenColour=="grey" then
            colour=givenColour
        endif
    endprocedure
endclass
```

(1 mark for attribute Colour; 1 mark each for a constructor and attribute changeColour; 3 marks for ensuring that the only colours the dog can be changed to are black, brown, white or grey)

Chapter 7

1 A utility is a small program with one purpose, usually related to the upkeep of the system. (1 mark)

2 An area of secondary storage is used as virtual memory. (1 mark) Pages not immediately necessary are moved into virtual memory. These pages are then copied back to physical memory when they are required. (1 mark)

3 When an interrupt signal is generated, the CPU first completes its current fetch–decode–execute cycle. (1 mark) If the interrupt is of a higher priority than the current process, the contents of the CPU's registers are stored in a stack in memory. (1 mark) The location of the appropriate interrupt service routine (ISR) is loaded into the program counter. (1 mark) When the ISR has finished running, the top of the stack is popped and the contents loaded into the registers. (1 mark)

4 The shortest-job-first algorithm can lead to starvation. (1 mark) If shorter jobs keep being generated, then a larger job may never get processed. (1 mark)

5 Running off a virtual machine adds an extra layer of processing. The virtual machine has to execute the intermediate code but then the CPU is executing the virtual machine executing the intermediate code. (1 mark) This results in code that runs more slowly than it would directly from the CPU. (1 mark)

6 Closed-source software tends to be widely used and so help is widely available. (1 mark) Often paid support is available from the company that produced it. (1 mark)

Chapter 8

1 Compilers and assemblers both convert source code to machine code. (1 mark) The difference is that a compiler converts high-level code, whereas an assembler converts low-level (assembly) code. (1 mark)

2 Programmers might use an interpreter whilst coding a program. Interpreters can make debugging easier as there is no need to wait for compilation (1 mark) and they show errors as they are encountered when the code is run. (1 mark)

3 During lexical analysis, comments and white space are removed from the source code. (1 mark) The code is turned to a series of tokens with details of variables and subroutines stored in a symbol table. (1 mark)

4 A loader is part of the operating system than loads a program being run and associate libraries into memory. (1 mark)

Chapter 9

1 Failure to carry out a feasibility study may result in a project being started that fails before completion. (1 mark) This may be for a number of reasons, such as there not being enough time or money available, or the project not being technically possible to implement. (1 mark)

2 Beta testing allows the software to be tested outside of the company. (1 mark) This is useful as bugs can be discovered when software is used in ways the developers didn't intend and is used on new hardware configurations. (1 mark)

3 The purpose of technical documentation is to provide the necessary information to allow the system to be maintained (1 mark) and updated in the future. (1 mark)

4 Extreme programming (XP) is focused around quality code. Code is written in pairs (1 mark), regularly refactored (made more efficient whilst retaining functionality) (1 mark), with every programmer having responsibility for all the code. (1 mark)

5 The waterfall lifecycle is poorly suited to risky projects. If a problem is discovered during coding it may be necessary to go back several stages to correct, if it is possible to correct at all. (1 mark) This could be after the investment of large amounts of time and money. (1 mark) The spiral lifecycle aims to identify and resolve the highest risks early on in the process (1 mark) before too many resources have been invested. (1 mark)

Chapter 10

1 As it has no moving parts, flash memory is unaffected by sudden movements (as may be likely on a mobile phone). (1 mark)

It consumes less power than mechanical hard drives. (1 mark)

2 The address bus carries the memory address that data is being written to or read from. (1 mark)

3 Two from:
- CISC has a wider range of instructions than RISC. (1 mark)
- RISC instructions take few (usually one) clock cycles to complete, whereas RISC take several. (1 mark)
- CISC has more addressing modes than RISC. (1 mark)
- CISC processors have more transistors than RISC processors. (1 mark)

4 The Von Neumann architecture uses a single control unit and arithmetic logic unit. (1 mark) It follows the fetch–decode–execute cycle. (1 mark) Data and instructions are stored together in memory. (1 mark)

(1 mark for each point up to a maximum of 2)

5 A GPU or graphics processing unit is a processor with an instruction set specifically designed for calculations used in 3D graphics. (1 mark) It has multiple ALUs and so is able to apply the same instruction to multiple pieces of data simultaneously. (1 mark)

Chapter 11

1 (a) 10111100 (2 marks, 1 per nibble)

(b) BC (2 marks, 1 per digit)

2 It provides a shorthand for those who work in binary that is simpler to understand and remember. (1 mark)

It is easy to make a mistake entering large binary numbers while the hexadecimal equivalent is much easier to remember and less likely to be entered incorrectly. (1 mark)

Hexadecimal is convenient because making direct conversion between binary and hexadecimal is straightforward. (1 mark)

3 (a) 11110000 (2 marks, 1 per nibble)

(b) 10010000 (2 marks, 1 per nibble)

4 (a) Colour depth (1 mark), resolution (1 mark), image size. (1 mark)

(b) Three from: Sample rate, bit depth, length of recording, number of channels. (3 marks)

5 It cannot distinguish between them superficially; it interprets what it finds according to the context of the program. (1 mark) If it expects to find an instruction, it will attempt to execute it; if it expects data, it will treat it as data.

Chapter 12

1 101 (Working, including carry digits, must be shown for 2 marks)

2

47 –	00101111
1's comp	11010000
Add 1	11010001
72 =	01001000
Add (1)	00011001

(5 marks, 1 per line)

3 –.025

(Working or explanation must be shown for 2 marks)

4 (a) 01010 011 (Working or explanation must be shown for 2 marks)

(b) 01000 010 (Working or explanation must be shown for 2 marks)

(c) 01011 001 (Working or explanation must be shown for 2 marks)

5 In the first four places all values are set to 1; in the last four bits, they are left as they were.

1	0	1	1	0	1	1	0	operand
1	1	1	1	0	0	0	0	mask
1	1	1	1	0	1	1	0	OR

(2 marks, 1 for masked output, 1 for comment)

Chapter 13

1 (a)

Start pointer 3		
Index	**Data**	**Pointer**
1	5	2
2	7	4
3	2	5
4	8	0
5	4	1
6		

(3 marks, 1 for start pointer, 2 for correct pointers [1 if one mistake])

(b)

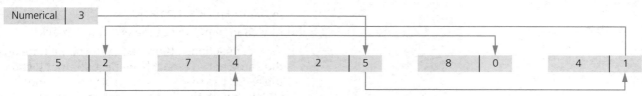

(2 marks for all arrows correct, 1 if one mistake, bonus mark for free pointer list)

(c)

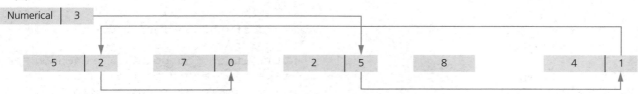

(2 marks; if you have added 4 to the free pointer list, award yourself a bonus mark)

2

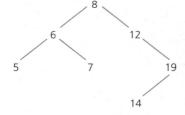

(3 marks, 1 for each level correct below the root note)

3

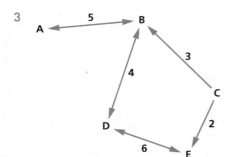

(3 marks, 1 for arrows correctly placed, 1 for arrows pointing in the correct direction, 1 for correct weightings)

4

Stack									
			C		E				
		B	B	B	B	B		D	
	A	A	A	A	A	A	A	A	A
Visited	A	B	C		E			D	

Queue									
	A	A	A						
		B	B	B	B	B			
			D	D	D	D	D		
				C	C	C	C		
					E	E	E	E	
Current	A	A	A	B	B	B	D	C	E
Visited	A	B	D		C	E			

(8 marks, 4 for each table, 1 for the columns from each visited node to the next visited node)

5 85 (Working must be shown for 2 marks)

Chapter 14

1 (a) ¬A ∧ ¬B ∧ (A ∨ C)

  ¬A ∧ A = 0

  Therefore:

  ¬A ∧ B ∧ C

  ¬A ∧ ¬B ∧ C (3 marks, 1 for answer, 2 for working)

 (b) (B ∧ C) ∧ (B ∨ C) = (B ∧ C)

  (A ∧ B) ∨ (B ∧ C) (2 marks)

 (c) (A ∧ B) ∨ C (1 mark)

Chapter 15

1 (a) Answers are examples only, and are not definitive.

```
TblClient
ClientRef
Client_Name
Client_Phone

TblAnimal
Animal_Ref
Animal_Name
Client_Ref
Treatment_Ref
Date_Next_Due

TblTreatment
Treatment_Ref
Treatment_name
```

(6 marks, 1 for any data item – there should be two from each of the three tables)

(b)

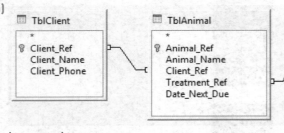

(6 marks)

(c) Example SQL (syntax may vary in different versions):

```
SELECT "TblClient"."Client_Name",
"TblClient"."Client_Phone",
"TblTreatment"."Treatment_Name",
"TblAnimal"."Animal_Name",
"TblAnimal"."Date_Next_Due",
"TblAnimal"."Animal_Name" FROM
"TblAnimal", "TblTreatment",
"TblClient" WHERE
"TblAnimal"."Treatment_Ref" =
"TblTreatment"."Treatment_Ref" AND
"TblAnimal"."Client_Ref" =
```

"TblClient"."Client_Ref" AND
"TblAnimal"."Date_Next_Due" =
{D '2016-04-03'}

(1 mark for each SQL command term and 1 mark for each correct field selected, to a maximum of 3)

2 Data redundancy is unnecessary (1 mark) repetition of data. (1 mark) Data integrity is data as it should be/accurate (1 mark); it reflects reality. (1 mark)

3 (a) The database is consistent. (1 mark) There are no conflicts between data stored in different tables. (1 mark)

 (b) Table of exams.
  Table of students.
  Table of exam entries.
  Referential integrity will not allow the deletion of exam data (1 mark) if it is being referenced by exam entries. (1 mark)

4 (a) Any change in the database data. (1 mark)

 (b) Two transactions attempted at the same time on the same data. (1 mark) The first attempt locks the record so that the second attempt cannot interfere with the first transaction. (1 mark)

5 move to end of the file
 write new record to new file
 (4 marks)

6 start at the beginning of the file
 copy records to new file
 until insertion point is reached
 write new record to new file
 write remaining records from old file
 to new file
 (4 marks)

Chapter 16

1 Examples:
  - Interpose a firewall between the network and the outside. (2 marks)
  - Encrypt data in transmission. (2 marks)

2 (a) Each layer is concerned only with communicating (1 mark) with adjacent layers. (1 mark) Development/maintenance (1 mark) can be restricted to just a small part of the system. (1 mark)

  (b) Layer 1 (physical) is concerned with the carrying, sending and receiving of electrical signals. (1 mark) Layer 2 (data link) provides data frames suitable for placing on layer 1./ Detects errors. (1 mark)

  (c) • OSI has seven layers (1mark); TCP/IP has four layers. (1 mark)
      • TCP/IP application layer includes the OSI application layer, presentation layer, and most of the session layer. (1 mark)
      • TCP/IP transport layer includes the OSI session layer and the OSI transport layer. (1 mark)
      • The TCP/IP internet layer is a subset of the OSI network layer. (1 mark)
      • The TCP/IP link layer includes the OSI data link layer and the physical layers. (1 mark)

  (d) It is a concept to assist working rather than a reality. (1 mark) The reality is based on the concept. (1 mark)

3 It sends data packets (1 mark) to the next network/segment. (1 mark)

4 A set of rules (1 mark) or standards (1 mark) that dictate the operation of a network. (1 mark)

5 In packet switching, data is packaged into units called packets. (1 mark) Packets are sent via routers (1 mark), probably by different routes. (1 mark) The message is reassembled at the destination. (1 mark)

  Circuit switching is a dedicated fixed circuit (1 mark) that remains open throughout a data transmission session. (1 mark)

6

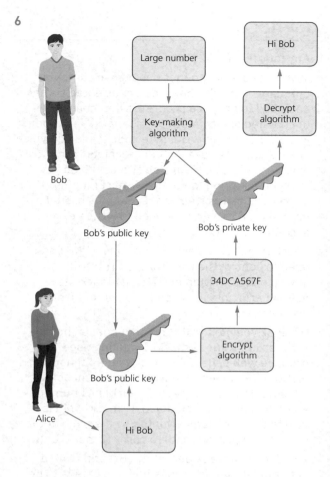

(6 marks)

THE CITY OF
LIVERPOOL COLLEGE
LRC

Chapter 17

1 Any four from:

Java is a compiled general-purpose computer language (1 mark) that is object oriented (1 mark) and used to produce programs that can run unchanged on any platform. (1 mark) Java code is compiled to generate byte code (1 mark), which can be run on a Java Virtual machine. (1 mark) JavaScript is an interpreted (1 mark) high-level untyped scripting language (1 mark) that is often used inside web pages and interpreted by browsers. It can also be used to write server-side scripts. (1 mark)

2 Cascading Style Sheets (1 mark) is a language used to control the presentation (1 mark) of web pages written in HTML. (1 mark) Its guiding principle is to separate content from presentation. (1 mark)

3 HTML (Hypertext Markup Language) is the standard markup (1 mark) language used to produce web pages. (1 mark) XML (Extensible Markup Language) defines rules for encoding documents in a web page (1 mark) in a human- and machine-readable form. (1 mark) XML is designed to use tags invented by the page author (that is, not pre-defined) to carry (1 mark) data.

4 The data is stored separately (1 mark) from a data model that describes how the data is to be reconstructed (1 mark) so a dictionary (1 mark) of words or other data can be stored with an indication of where the words (or data) are to be inserted in the reconstructed (uncompressed) file. (1 mark)

5 A spreadsheet (1 mark) and a computer program (1 mark). (In each case, any permanent loss of data would have an adverse impact on the uncompressed file.)

Topic 4

Chapter 18

1 Relevant provisions of DPA:
  1 Purpose must be revealed to the subject when data is collected – has this been done? (1 mark)
  2 Data should not be disclosed to other parties without permission – has this been sought? (1 mark)
  3 Data must not be transferred outside the UK unless adequate data protection legislation is in place – is the sister company outside the UK? (1 mark) Is there adequate data protection legislation if they are? (1 mark)

2 Possible themes:

Current employment (for example at an event whilst claiming illness, comments detrimental to the employer, ideas not acceptable to the employer) (1 mark)

Future employment (1 mark)

Illegal activity (location will be given) (1 mark)

Future social/friendship/family networks may see past activities (1 mark)

3 Ideas from the list on page 142:

Screen readers for the blind user, options for larger text or a screen magnifier, choice of font, audio description, contrasting colours for text and background, subtitles or a transcript for deaf users (All explained with examples for 6 marks)

4 Discussion to cover what the employer might see, why they might do this and whether it is acceptable that they do this (for 6 marks)

5 General use of monitoring including: CCTV, GPS tracking on phones, health and activity tracking on phones and other devices

Benefits of day-to-day monitoring: Many possible areas of benefit, including health tracking; locating people, friends and family; crime prevention; monitoring criminal and terrorist activity; manufacturers monitoring cars for issues in case of breakdown or for tracking down stolen vehicles

(6 marks for 6 separate points made)